IdeaClicks

IdeaClicks

All about innovation . . .

Santosh Deshmukh

PARTRIDGE
A Penguin Random House Company

Print History:
June 2014 First Edition.

To order additional copies of this book, contact
Partridge India
000 800 10062 62
orders.india@partridgepublishing.com

www.partridgepublishing.com/india

CONTENTS

Explains the importance of global innovation to make things simple and useful. Creates general awareness around innovation and helps you find smarter ways of doing things differently and making life easy and efficient. Presents an innovation model which can be adopted by any individual, organization or group to start the process of innovation. Helps you build the eco-system of Innovation to tap ideas from the grass root level and giving them life. Bring innovative minds together and harness the potential of teamwork in implementing ideas. Applicable for everyone and everywhere to take that first step towards solving basic human problem.

DEDICATION

To my wife who encouraged me to write down my five years of experience in form of a book.

To myself for taking those back paining efforts and taking this book towards completion.

To my parents who made the person that I am today.

To my late sister Vandana whose presence and motivation I miss so much.

ABOUT THE AUTHOR

The author is experienced software professional who has worked with multiple product based multinational companies. Through his experience working on different products and unmet market demands, he has developed more inclination towards innovation. To his credits he has three thousand plus followers on his Facebook page http://ww.facebook.com/IdeaClicks. He also actively drives an idea management portal http://www.IdeaClicks.in for bringing innovation from grass root level of the society.

He is an innovation maven and has been driving innovation programs at **PayPal** India office for more than five years. He is awarded with **PayPal / Labs - Innovator Award** presented by company Vice President Mr. Nik Sathe for his rigorous efforts towards supporting the innovation efforts at **PayPal**.

The author is also a certified scrum master and has been practicing Agile for more than ten years. He has a master degree in Computer Science from University of Pune, Maharashtra, India.

His Complete professional details can be found at: in.linkedin.com/in/santoshdeshmukh

ACKNOWLEDGEMENT

I would like to thank all of my colleagues who actively participated in the innovation programs. Stopped me wherever you could (including the loo) to make me listen to your mind blowing ideas. To my mentors who enriched my experience and trusted in me to carry the responsibility of driving the innovation programs.

Finally, thanks to all the innovators out there, who are keen on making this world a great place to live.

CHAPTER 1

Introduction & Awareness

There is an innovator in each one of us. The only thing is how soon we realize this and work on it, to make it a reality and become successful. It doesn't mean making profits or gaining popularity but definitely making someone's life easy and comfortable than what it was earlier.

As they say "CHOTA PACKET, BADA DHAMAKA"(small packet, bigger blast), Innovation has the same effect with smaller ideas. Each one of us has ideas. No idea is small or BIG. An idea is an idea. It can come at anytime, anywhere. No matter whether you are in a park, wash room, shopping in a mall, travelling or are at work. You can get ideas absolutely anywhere. You should make it a point to note them on a piece of paper, immediately. EUREKA? EUREKA? An idea can change your life!.

Usually people in a group or an organization come from different background, different geographies. Each one of them has his own experience and smart way of solving day-to-day problems. There is a need to tap this talent and help them innovate. Every organization should have an innovation ecosystem in place to help people be innovative and add value to the organization.

How about Homepage of a company website having "Innovation" tab similar to "Career", "AboutUs", "ContactUs" tabs which carries information related to various innovation programs present in the company.

> "You unnecessarily worry about things when your destiny is so well written."
>   - Santosh Deshmukh

How this book is structured

This book contains ten chapters. Initial 4 Chapters explain you Innovation Model which is a generic model that any individual or organization can adapt to start innovation.

From an Individual perspective, I will be explaining a step by step approach to follow and the different level of hurdles he need to cross, in order to take his idea to a successfully completion state.

From an organization or group's perspective, I will be explaining as to what all things it need to have in place (the ecosystem), so that it can invite ideas, filter the important ones, groom them and reward those that get successfully implemented.

People have ideas but don't know where to take them. Therefore, there needs to be a platform that can tap bright ideas and help the innovators build them. In case of unavailability of such a platform, ideas remain ideas or they get lost.

In this book, I am going to explain you the importance of innovation and create general awareness around it. After reading this book, I expect you to have a fair understanding about this topic and feel motivated to take the first step towards innovation. Encourage your friends and colleagues to innovate and get new ideas.

I am going to share some interesting examples of daily life innovation (some rather funny) which would catch your attention and make you cautiously notice things around.

I will also be sharing some motivational speeches from some great innovation leaders.

I will be sharing some avenues where you can submit ideas and make a difference.

Contests are catalysts that take your ideas to newer height. We will see different contests that can happen and how interesting it becomes when it goes beyond innovation and comes to creativity. Packaging your idea with presentations, voice recording, acting, mockups and videos. Also the importance and purpose of each contest type and its format. Share some details about tools that can help you prepare your demonstrations to participate in these contests.

As a case study, we will take a look at a Global Payments Company where we worked. How we started as volunteers to drive the innovation programs and how we grew to become innovation champions, motivating people and encouraging them to get more ideas.

The journey that we took, right from organization expressing its interest around Innovation, through a general communication email and few enthusiasts like us, sensing this as an opportunity and calling for a kick start meeting in which we decided to contribute in this initiative, till the ecosystem was completely built.

I will be explaining you the importance of idea germination, forming a group of passionate innovators, brainstorming ideas, sending regular NewsLetters with discussion points, having an email signature that displays your passion towards innovation, listening to people, token of appreciation for submitting new ideas etc.

I will also explain on how organizations can benefit by inviting ideas from employees in different categories. My references and examples would be much dependent on my personal experiences backed by solid instances to support them with real life examples.

This book answers following questions for an individual:

- I have an idea.
- What next
- Whom can I reach and discuss
- How do I know if its duplicate
- Can I write it some where
- Can I do some research around it and build it
- Can I talk to my friends or colleagues about this
- Can I present it to audience
- How to articulate it better
- Can I get feedback and incorporate comments
- Can I form a team and implement my idea
- Is it worth pursuing
- What's the reward

This book answers following questions for an organization:

- We as leaders do not have answers to all the problems
- We are interested in collecting ideas
- What should be the first step
- Should we seek people opinion
- Are there certain areas in which we are interested
- Do we need Idea Management Portal

- Do we need a maven who can drive this
- Does it need management involvement
- Do we need separate Innovation and Research department
- Can we also look for patenting
- Do we need Recognition and Rewards
- How will this help the organization

Who should read this book

- Buddying innovators who have ideas and wish to take that first step and succeed as an innovator. Who wish to make their ideas click
- Organizations, Universities or Groups who wish to benefit from innovation and bring in a culture of innovation. Who wish to grow and explore new horizons by means of Innovation.

CHAPTER 2

Everyone can innovate

Floating Pencil (Levitating Pencil) : Gift received by Std VI student Abhishek Shinde for participating and standing second in Sir C V Raman BalVaidnyanik exam conducted in Ahamednagar Dist of Maharashtra state, India.

If wearing a watch on the other hand gives you a WOW feeling, you are Innovative. It is as simple as this. Anything that saves you money, time or effort is Innovation. Anything that brings effectiveness, reliability is Innovation. Anything that makes things simple is Innovation. We should try to solve basic human problem by means of simple and effective solutions that would appeal for the masses. A simple effective alternative to existing thing is innovation. Any disruptive thought that changes the way people think or work, is Innovation. Anything that is smart is Innovation. It can happen to anyone, anywhere, any field, any region. You don't need to be a genius to be an innovator.

Innovation can happen in any field: Hotel industry, social innovation, manufacturing, industrial process, daily labor work, home innovation, medical innovation, health care innovation, engineering innovation, technical innovation, government process innovation, town planning, traffic management, transport, agriculture, urban innovation, rural innovation and the list goes on. There is so much of opportunity around and different areas where we can innovate.

A big picture of your idea can be as big as building the success story of Amul (Anand Milk Udyog Ltd) a milk cooperative in Anand district of Gujrat state in India. Or it can be something like a matrimonial website which serves millions of people and take away their worries in finding the right match for their loved ones. But defining milestones is important and ensuring every small step in achieving them is definitely taken. Innovation is more successful when there is a cooperative participation and team effort. There are certain exceptions where individuals have on their own created success stories.

Everyone can be innovative. Everyone has smarter ways of doing things. Innovation is anything that changes your perspective of not looking at things in the same old way and following them as they were set initially.

There is always a scope for us to improve in everything that we do in our daily life. Every one of us is creative. If you see around, you would notice there are multiple such innovative things present.

To explain the importance of wearing a seat belt while driving a car, a company came up with an innovative way of asking people to sit inside

the car and making the car upside down using a crane. Would people understand this if you tell them politely?

Earlier cars like ambassador and fiat use to have a small window flap in the front which you could use to get some fresh breeze. The same way auto rickshaw drivers copied this technique knowingly or unknowingly and started using cardboards to feel the breeze in the scorching sun. There is an opportunity for the auto designers right? Sometimes we fail to notice such fantastic things.

Someone in Punjab started using washing machine for preparing lassi when demand for his milk based drink increased. At times completely new solution works but sometimes small but incremental changes also matter a lot.

The great maratha king, Chatrapati Shivaji Maharaj had an innovative way of recognizing his commanders. Whoever killed more than 100 people in war, he would recognize them by embossing a golden star on their swords. One of his trusted sardaar, Hambirrao Mohite had six such golden stars on his sword. You can imagine the fear that it would create when one would stand in front of such a ferocious person.

A coal mine worker puts in hard effort to get the coal out and load it in trucks. Can we as an outsider reduce some of his hard labor? And make his life a little bit comfortable. Or whether he himself has to be creative and identify ways of making things differently and make his and his co-workers' life easy?

What about developers fixing some core dump or crash related live issue. Can any tool be helpful if it's a frequent issue?

A farmer came up with an innovative solution to start his water pump with mobile vibrator by giving it a miss call. He could now start and stop his water pump sitting at home, reducing his trips to his farm.

A person named "SANDWICH" was a gambler and couldn't find enough time from his gambling to eat the bread with the hot ingredients served in the plate.

To save time, he asked the chef to put the stuffing into the bread slices itself and serve him. This innovative food item is now called as Sandwich.

A techie working in Bangalore wanted to go home in Hyderabad for Diwali. He couldn't purchase the bus ticket and finally had to stay away from his family even during the festive season. He just couldn't digest the fact and worked on solving this problem. Thus online bus booking system RedBus was born.

To increase profit and sales some toothpaste companies came up with an innovative solution to increase the diameter of the tube outlet, so that people start consuming more. This is ofcourse cunning but yeah, it's an idea.

Here are my words of wisdom:

Stay optimistic about your ideas and creativity.

Keep thinking deeply and note down ideas that come to your mind. But don't lose the interest on the initial ones.

Don't get demotivated if someone has already thought about this earlier. There could be a scope to enhance it further. What if Nokia®, Blackberry® were once the global leader in making sturdy mobile phones, SAMSUNG® and HTC® could still capture the market with their Android® based smart phones.

Keep yourself motivated and reach out to people who like hearing your ideas.

Me and my wife were taking an evening beach walk after work and she happen to tell me that she always wondered on "Why clockwise? Can't the clocks run anticlock?". To be honest this idea struck my mind and I felt for amusement purpose it would be really appealing, especially to the younger and rebellious generation. We then starting thinking on its design change and possible ways to make this happen. I suggested having dial on both sides and the common mechanism in the middle layer. So there will be two hour hands on each side of the mechanism. Two min hands on each side of the mechanism. And two seconds hands on each side of the mechanism. Now when you place this dial on your wrist and if it's running clockwise, then try to flip it upside down and you would notice it runs anticlock also. Jaadoo!!! (magic) Isn't it!

Well, we took this idea to the Design head of one of the biggest watch brand in India. He simply said "It's not possible because there would be a huge design change and the mechanism that we would build would shoot the price of the watch". Would you agree?

It's pretty simple, if watches can run clockwise, they can also be made to run anticlock. No?

In fact there is already a patent filed in Canada for watches to run with anti-clock design.

That's the beauty. When you think out of the box and come up with new way of doing things, the exceptionally expert person would probably reject your idea with solid reasons. No offense. He has all the valid reasons to say "Your ideas won't work". But you as an aggressive innovator have to challenge yourself and to the world and prove that your idea is possible. Change the rules of the world.

Be crazy about your idea. It's best to be a child than being an adult in the game of innovation. Cause a child is fearless of failure or falling down. It's mind always has questions and curious to know more.

100 ideas will come to your mind, list down and focus on those which you feel would click.

> **"Dream is not what you see in sleep, dream is the thing which does not let you sleep." –President of India Dr. A.P.J. Abdul Kalam**

Innovation model

Innovation is the BUZZWORD these days and you would find its mention in various NEWS articles and companies' headlines. Everyone wants to be innovative and outsmart the competitors. The reason is obviously because of the competitiveness in market demand and rapidly changing technology. To keep yourself in the fast paced race, one has to keep trying new things and get rid of old ways of doing things.

So, this appears to be a common challenge for individuals as well as organizations and hence there needs to be a generic **innovation model** which can help them set things fast and give them a quick perspective about this BUZZ around and guide them in setting up things to get started with the process of innovation. There's no point in everybody experiencing the same initial challenges in setting up things for collecting ideas and investing time when someone already has spent enough time and defined a pattern that suites your requirement.

The objective is to define "Innovation Model" which is a generic model which Individuals or organizations can adapt and quickly start idea creation. Once you have a pool of ideas, you can find ways to take them forward.

CHAPTER 3

Individual perspective

Add life to your idea:

- Innovators have lot of ideas: Since every individual come from a different background and carry unique experience, each one of us have ideas that are different. We are able to relate different things and identify pain points, which if addressed up on, can create a positive impact.

- Note it down on a piece of paper: Recording your ideas is very important as there are chances of you forgetting them and who knows, these ideas potentially could be a game changer. Unless the idea is present in front of you in a physical form, there are fewer chances that you would work on it and implement it to completion.

- See if similar idea already exists: You are not the only one who can get ideas around a certain topic. It's possible that someone else is also thinking on the same lines. It's always god to teamup and implement your idea successfully. You shouldn't really carry the fear of who takes the credit, instead measure your confidence level after your idea is live. The Reward of being successful is much greater than anything else.

- Search on the internet and build some supportive material around it: You need to do a lot of research around your idea and try to gather as much information as possible. This will help you in understanding if there are already any attempts made around this and whether you need to be aware of certain failures. Internet is a boon where information that people share reaches every corner of the world and someone's prior efforts might save your time in a big way.

- Work on it to make it concrete: Try to close possible gaps in your idea and see if there is a flawless connection between all the execution points of your idea.

- Talk to people and see if it appeals to them and they would buy your idea: Sometimes we feel very pumped up and without taking to our end user or customer, we just go building it only to find the fundamental is missing. Never do this. Engage your customer and seek their feedback right from start of your idea implementation.

- See if you can build a prototype yourself: Prototype is important as it shuts down all blabbering around and straight way demonstrates your idea.

- Talk to people and see if they can contribute: Having an idea and actually implementing it are two farther points. One need to passionately drive his idea and regularly follow on it to take it to completion. Due to daily work pressures, it's not always possible to dedicatedly spare time and make progress on your idea. Therefore, it's good to identify champions who can contribute and help you taking your idea forward.

- Seek feedback and keep incorporating it: As you discuss your idea with different people and involve them, you keep getting feedback which you need to note very meticulously and religiously follow up on addressing it. This would build trust amongst the people and in turn they would be happy to experience the product or outcome of your idea. Your sincere and transparent approach would earn you trusted customers who would help you climb the success ladder quickly.

- List down use cases to make it complete: It's very important to get your hands dirty in building a prototype of your idea and seek first hand feedback from end user. You should not stop here, if your prototype is ready. Leave no stone unturned and try to cover all possible scenarios around your idea. In some cases your idea might not have multiple scenarios but there will always be a scope to increase its usability or effectiveness.

- Find out ways to advertise it: You should be the brand ambassador of your idea. Don't be shy to advertise it by means that are not offensive but ones those are acceptable by the audience and working.

- Wet your idea with legal, compliance, ethics teams to ensure your work is acceptable: Sometimes we don't bother much about legal and ethicalness of our idea. Whether it will be accepted and not be damaging to the society. It's important to think on these lines as it affects your reputation as an innovator. Next time you have an idea, people will definitely carry this thought while giving you their feedback.

- Check with intellectual property law firms in your country if it can be patentable or considered as an extension to existing ideas: There are certain law firms that deal with patenting ideas. With a fees, they help you search if such an idea is already patented. If not they help you through the patenting process. At times, your idea is an extension to existing idea and a separate patent can be filed for the same.

- Don't worry about return on investment at the beginning

- Keep improvising your idea: What we call baking your idea. Keep refining it, polishing it, using crisp words, till it becomes catchy. This goes to a state where people are able to understand your idea in first few minutes of your pitch.

- Explore avenues where you can present your idea: Your idea becomes HOT when there is more and more social acceptance to it. People are talking about it and importantly it's working. So, explore avenues where you can participate and present your idea and create a BUZZ about your idea.

- Give a free hand to champions if they are ready to publicize it: If you are able to connect with champions who are willing to sell your idea and market it, do not interfere or cut them at any point. Let them promote your idea.

Submit Ideas

Everybody has ideas. Move them forward through different phases of idea cycle. Bake them and prepare a prototype of it so that it becomes ready for implementation. There are ideas which get rejected by judges but because of the passion and belief of the individuals these ideas find way in daily usage of people. Some work on their ideas while some just sit on it.

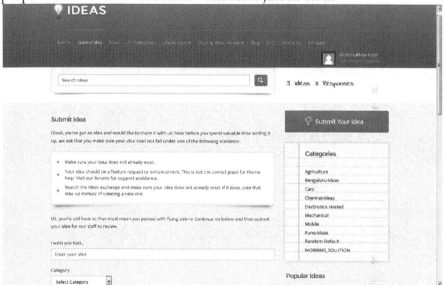

Moving Ideas Forward

Idea can be submitted in a very raw state. This is to make sure your claim of being the first one to have the prior art. You can then phrase your idea in appropriate words and format mentioning problem statement, proposed solution and business gain. After these initial steps it becomes very important to **"Move Your Idea Forward"** by socializing it, promoting with your network and capturing right attention by collecting votes. Discussing your ideas with fellow coworkers and seeking their feedback to shape your idea and make it **BUZZWORTHY**.

Here we explain on Baking Ideas, grooming them. Search for similar ideas and group up with people. Work on finding references, study materials and internet information. Talk to people and seek their opinion on improving the quality of your ideas. The initial thought that you had in your mind could be just 5%(tip of the iceberg) of the complete resulting product that shape up. Keep researching and collecting as much material around your idea as you can. Make your idea BUZZ worthy by collecting more votes and comments. Keep answering and documenting to queries that come up in the discussions. If you just have plans and cannot really implement, hunt and team up with people who can implement your idea, at least till creating a POC and getting funding. Don't stop here, be creative and come up with different use cases and design proposals.

You must seek feedback which says 3 good things they liked about your idea. 3 things which they did not like about your idea. And 3 things which they feel needs to be captured or improved in your idea. Do not take any comment personally or get demotivated by harsh comments. Instead look for this as an opportunity and position your idea in such a way that the core of your idea still remains the same but the packaging and wrapping words capture most of the audience.

Completeness

Innovation should be think through completely and possible use cases and parameters should be accessed in a holistic manner.

Henry Ford came with a beautiful innovation product, a car which nobody in those days had even thought of. If he would have asked people what they want, probably people might have asked for horses that run faster. But he carefully observed the need and came up with a revolutionary product that changed the definition of luxury and mobility. The Car.

But did you know that the first car that he built, did not have a reverse gear? That does not demerit the actual innovation that he did, may be because that was not felt as a necessity during those times but definitely if you think now it becomes a primary requirement of any modern car. Point here is to have a holistic approach in what you think, what you do and continuously keep improvising it.

It's not that we are done with all the primary necessity that one expects in a vehicle. We still have exceptions in some areas.

- What if a beautiful lady is driving to some ceremony with all her make up, jewelry, carefully worn costume and all of a sudden her vehicle brakes down on a crowded traffic signal? The traffic cop suddenly comes and asks her to pull her vehicle to the side to avoid blocking and there is no one to help?

- Or you are a novice driver and want to park your vehicle in a much narrow slot which you are afraid you might rub to a wall or another vehicle if you use a normal clutch or accelerator.

- Or you are stuck in a slow moving traffic and you don't want to trouble your ignition every now and then but still keep your vehicle moving as the vehicles move with snail's pace.

- You are in middle of traffic, it's raining heavily with roads flooded and your vehicle unable to start the engine.

Don't you think that there should be a hand brake kind of lever using which you can move your vehicle backward and forward without actually starting the engine?

The lady should be able to pull her vehicle off the road still sitting inside the car. No push required, no getting wet in the rain, no inconvenience to others. Well this may come true say ten years from now but things like these should be thought through as much as possible.

So, it becomes extremely important to think through all possible use cases of your idea and make it as much generic as possible to be accepted globally. One must come out of time and location boundaries. Of course every idea takes its own time to mature and become complete but the credit goes to the innovator if the proposal is thought through from all possible angles, leaving any scope for improvement or modifications. You become more confident about your idea and people whom you discuss with get the sense of completeness and get driven by your thoughts almost instantly.

Innovation can be disastrous at times, if it's not thought through completely.

Mistakes like these are still repeating.

The latest shared auto rickshaw that we see plying on city roads doesn't have a starter button or key to start the engine.

One has to get down of the vehicle and with help of a rope, rotate the engine wheel that is located at the rear portion, to start the vehicle.

And that's the primary reason these auto rickshaw driver do not switch off their engines on traffic signals where they can possibly save on some precious fuel.

More over these auto rickshaw's do not have a handbrake to keep the vehicle firm at one place.

So if the auto is on a small slope and the driver has to get down to start the engine with the rope, then the vehicle starts rolling on the slope unless there is any other person who can sit on the driver seat for some time and hold the brake paddle till the time the auto driver starts the engine manually.

What if all the passengers are ladies or old people who are not much comfortable doing this?

What a funny design and I am surprised on how Automobile Research Authority approved its design.

Attend weekly brain storming session

Individuals should participate in the weekly idea grooming sessions.

These sessions are meant for creating general innovation awareness, motivating people and directing them towards appropriate references. This has a catalyst effect which helps in generating more ideas and bringing innovative minds together, thereby benefiting mutually. These sessions help people participate and present their ideas in front of larger audience from different cross vertical teams. These are preparatory and practice sessions that help innovators to get early feedback on their ideas. There are no restrictions as to how many times the same idea can be presented. The day and time of the session is decided after consulting people and meticulously considering their priorities and concerns. We opted for Thursday since many people prefer taking leave on Monday or Friday to avail a long weekend break. Tuesday and Wednesday was ruled out due to the focus on core working hours. Thursday, people are in much control of their activities and can manage to spend some time for innovation. Why 2PM? Well that's the time after lunch when people are relaxed and in a mood to absorb new thoughts. People criticize, acclaim, suggest alternatives, fill in gaps on the ideas that you present.

Video making

A video of 3-4 four minutes. You can create one with actual people or you can opt for animation. There are many online software available these days like **"powtoons.com"** which helps you in building an animated video very quickly. CamStudio and Camtasia are other tools using which you can create desktop screen recordings.

Why Video and not actual person talking? Well, you need to revisit and revamp your videos atleast 100+ times to make it fit for the 3 minutes time span and make that special impact on the judges. Generally judges or the audience get bored too quickly if you go around beating the bush and keep explaining the same thing again and again. You lose most of your time in "you know", "I mean" and your 3-4 minutes time just runs away and you are left with no special impression on the audience. You may also feel nervous if you are not good at public speaking. Hence video is a good option on which people can work on it to make it more crisp and perfect to the audience taste.

Remember Steve Jobs created Apple Macintosh Ad - Aired during the SuperBowl 1984?

Link: https://www.youtube.com/watch?v=8UZV7PDt8Lw

A big screen displaying army personnel marching and a lady athlete coming running from the audience and throwing the hammer towards the screen to break it into pieces. And this followed by a message "On January 24th, Apple Computer will introduce Macintosh. And you'll see why 1984 won't be like 1984".

What an impact it created on the audience towards Apple. So don't just create a video, create an impact with a video.

Your video should cover following:

1. Problem statement or pain point of your customer. Customer can be internal or external who uses your product or service.
2. Proposed solution
3. Benefits of implementing your solution
4. What if your proposed solution is not implemented

South Korea's S Oil HERE balloon campaign

Link: http://www.youtube.com/watch?v=nw9g9OVHdJI

This was the initiative to save on fuel which otherwise is wasted in finding a parking in an open parking ground. The idea was simple to keep a hydrogen filled balloon in the parking lot, which goes down when a car gets parked and goes up when the parking lot becomes vacant. People were able to spot the yellow color HERE balloon and could easily find a nearby parking slot.

Piano like musical steps at railway platform created amusement amongst tired passengers.

Link: https://www.youtube.com/watch?v=2lXh2n0aPyw

This was rather a funny idea to change the mindset of people the way they look at things. People who were shy of using the stairs and preferred the escalators in a subway were now attracted towards using the stairs since they were musical. They didn't just like climbing them but also enjoyed going up and down few times.

Toastmasters club

It's a great way to enhance and polish your public speaking skills. Toastmasters is an internationally recognized leader in communication and leadership development of individuals. Your organization needs to make necessary arrangements to form a toastmasters club. Your HR should help you in this regard. Volunteers should then take the ownership of running the Toastmasters sessions where a group of people assemble and speak on table topics or prepared speeches. Evaluator evaluates and identifies the number of pauses, fillers, body language in your speech. This helps individuals grow confident on their presentation skills and is quite helpful while pitching their ideas in front of the audience. You select crisp and meaningful wording while pitching your ideas and make maximum utilization of idea presentation time. If you are able to create an impact in first 10 seconds of your presentation, you stand to be the winner. On the contrary, even if your idea is mind blowing but you are unable to catch the attention of the audience, you fail. Many of the engineers come from a background where they do not have much exposure to the English language but are very good in Mathematics, Science and logical reasoning.

Toastmasters help these engineers to overcome fear and give a polished touch to their personality in public speaking.

Link: http://www.toastmasters.org

> **"No pain in the wounds received in the moment of victory"**
> **–Napoleon Bonaparte**

Take away

Being Innovative, You develop a new perspective towards life. So you no longer continue doing dull jobs. Instead look for opportunities to revamp existing things and bring in effective solutions.

> **"If you want a thing done well, do it yourself." -Napoleon Bonaparte**

CHAPTER 4

Organization perspective

Invite ideas

Organizations that realize the importance of innovation, take quick steps and reach to their employees and business partners in inviting ideas to make smart changes that are beneficial to the organization.

This shows the willingness and seriousness of the organization to embrace change and stay fit in the competitive race.

Organization can invite ideas in different areas of operations.

GoGreen: Power saving, water saving, employees' travel time to work, carpooling.

Operation Excellence: Saving time required for development / testing / build, saving hardware / software resources.

Corporate social responsibility: Donation related idea.

Initiatives like these improves employee engagement and addresses attrition rate to a certain extend. Thereby it lifts the morale and enables employees to implement whatever plans they have, to make their work place, better.

Leaders generally do not have all the answers and the best answers can come from employees as they are the subject matter experts in their area.

They can accurately say what skills are necessary in implementing these ideas and what all learnings they can contribute to.

This should help organizations create products desirable to the end users.

Tapping bright ideas

It becomes very important for an organization to systematically record ideas.

India had a gurukula system (type of school in India, residential in nature, with pupils (shishya) living near the guru, often within the same house) of education where all the knowledge which use to be with the guru was passed to pupils by verbal means only.

It was not recorded in any form. Casteism also was one of the reasons behind not recording the learnings and keeping the information only with the vital few.

Does anybody knows what all tricks in archery did guru Drona teach Arjuna to make him the best archer during the Mahabharata times ?

Eklavya who secretly tried to learn archery lessons that guru Drona taught to the princes was caught once and was asked to sacrifice his thumb (used for holding arrow with the string) as a guru dakshina (fees for his learnings).

Guru Drona ensured that his learnings are not passed to people whom he did not consider from the warrior linage.

Had those lessons been recorded, India would have had pool of Olympic medal winners in archery and shooting.

Even the historical physician like Sushruta from the 6th century BC in Varanasi, who use to practice plastic surgery, caesarian section in those ancient days, could not pass on his techniques as they were not recorded.

Therefore, recording your ideas, techniques, learning is important.

Idea management portal

- Vote for your favorite idea
- Submit your ideas here
- Earn rewards
- How do I move my idea forward?

This is idea management software. Portal plays a very important role in streamlining the process of innovation and facilitating people to submit their ideas as and when it strikes their mind. This portal should be easy to access for users at any time. There are quite good companies that help you setup this portal. BEST option is to create your own portal for your organization. With your login credentials, you should be able to login to this portal and use different functionalities.

These are some of the options you can try:

1. Microsoft Sharepoint Site: You can create your own ideation portal using Microsoft sharepoint site Ref: http://blogs.realdolmen.com/experts/2012/07/24/basic-ideationwith- sharepoint-and-project-online Or Search for "basic ideation with sharepoint and project online" on the web.

2. Word Wide Website: Search for webapp "Ideas Themes" that are available on the internet for a price. Download them in zip format, modify or customize the content as per your needs and upload them on your webhosting space or intranet server.

   Ref: http://ideas.appthemes.com

3. Word Wide Website: Create your amazon cloud space (Ref aws. amazon.com which is freely available for a year), upload your webapp (as explained in #2) and link your domain name to it.

4. Word Wide Website: Create your own NodeJS application and host it on webhosting space or intranet server

5. Idea Box: And finally the simplest option of all where there is no internet or electronics available, "Idea Box" which can be made out of a cardboard box and placed at common place where people can drop their ideas written on a piece of paper.

Following are the features an idea management portal should have:

- Web based and easy to access through internet browsers like IE, Chrome and Firefox.
- Capability to create your profile with a nice smiling photograph of yours.
- Capability to "Post New Ideas"
- Capability to "Search Existing Ideas" with a keyword or tags or filter criteria

- Capability to "Browse Existing Ideas",
  - o Vote positively or negatively against these ideas
  - o Add Comment and respond to existing comments
  - o Vote positively or negatively to each comment
- Capability to "View Existing Ideas" with modified idea displayed at top as latest modified. Every idea that is kept updated with important content should get proper attention from the audience by showcasing it in the latest updated list.
- CheckBox for idea submitters to mark idea as possible candidate for filing a patent
- Should contain leadership board tab to showcase top contributors and active members
- BLOG section for members to write blogs on their experience on innovation
  - o Normally BLOGS would some time contain FAQs for new members to find directions on commonly encountered problems
- Rewards section to reward members with certain gift items or for members to cash-in their reward points as per their choice
- Mechanism to calculate reward points for every contribution of members
  - o If you vote, you should get watts
  - o If you review existing ideas and comment on it, you should get watts
  - o If you write BLOGS (relevant to innovation) you should get watts
  - o In some cases administrator should be able to give watts to members for extra ordinary effort or participation
- Showcase different categories under which an idea can be submitted
- Showcase my profile page with a consolidated view of my personal idea submission and other activities that I perform
- Capability to add connections with other members and build your personal network of likeminded folks who would entertain your innovation thoughts and get notified of your activities

- Administrator should be able to define events on this portal and invite ideas related to the event

- Checkbox while submitting an idea for marking it as possible candidate for patent

---

"Even if you're on the right track, you'll get run over if you just sit there."

-Will Rogers

LABS facility

An independent, isolated from company network and work area, well-equipped LAB / facility which proves itself to be the center point of attraction for all the innovation and research related activities. It should facilitate idea presentation sessions and should have necessary hardware and software for implementing these ideas. People should feel carefree by keeping their work environment behind. They should feel enlightened the moment they enter this jazzy place. Catchy things like robots should be placed here which will give a WOW feeling to people who enter in to such facility. It should present your company's muscle power in the field of innovation and research. People would interact with like minded folks and here they would get to know so many other people from different cross vertical teams. Get to know tons of information flowing from the audience. Mere presence should benefit people with latest trends and technology in the market and new business needs. This should serve as a pit-stop for people to charge themselves with valuable information and experience. Anyone who wants to build an experience around a product and wants to receive first hand feedback from end users should be dying to show case his skills here to the audience. This place should serve as a magnet in attracting innovative minds and creating a vibrant facility for discussing all about ideas. There also should be space for presenters to come and practice for their presentations before-hand. A stage, full size mirror where people can actually work on their body language and fine tuning their presentation skills. The location of this place should be decided very carefully, especially companies which are spread across different sites where people might have to spend time in shuttling between these sites.

An ideal environment should have:

- A presentation desk with laptop
- Wifi connectivity that gives access to intra/inter net
- Sound system with mic to play innovation videos
- Projector with video conferencing capabilities
- Comfortable sitting arrangements for audience
- Windows, UNIX, Mac machines
- iPad, iPhone, Android smart phones
- Devices for scanning QR code and other hardware
- Phone extension for facilitating conference calls

Weekly NewsLetter

Create a weekly NewsLetter containing details of Ideas presented in the weekly brain storming session and send it to the internal innovation community. This way you keep people abreast of the latest updates and ideas presented during the ideation session. This ensures flow of information to folks even to those who have missed to attend the session due to some unavoidable situations. Showcasing the idea presenters photograph in the NewsLetter encourages the participants. You can also list down previously presented ideas to keep the BUZZ on. You can also highlight some interesting things happening outside your organization eg NewsPaper article excerpts. Or you can highlight some important announcements within the organization. Creativity is the limit to create a good NewsLetter. You should probably seek help of the communication team in your organization to come up with a neat formatted and grammatically correct NewsLetter.

Patents

Patenting an idea is very important. Every organization should have their own patent office which would help innovators in the patent process from start till successfully filing of the patent. If this is not feasible, then necessary tie up with an external third party who has expertise in this area would be beneficial. There should be a provision while submitting ideas to indicate whether it is a possible candidate for a patent.

As a reference www.giipinfo.com can be mentioned as one of external avenue where people can refer for Patent filing and knowledge on IP and Patent rights.

Global Institute of Intellectual Property (GIIP) is a leading Intellectual Property (IP) training company, co-headquartered at New Delhi, India and San Jose, USA. The company has been set up by a team of successful entrepreneurs, IP attorneys, patent agents and practitioners. GIIP provides training services covering IP generation, protection, commercialization and management.

GIIP aims to identify the brightest technical talent available in India and to train them in the best Intellectual Property (IP) techniques & practices available worldwide, to ultimately create a pool of elite IP professionals. These skilled professionals are trained to manage and lead the different IP functions & requirements of an Organization. GIIP has successfully graduated 400+ professionals from the Post Graduate Diploma & Certificate programs, in IP Rights (IPR) and Patent Management, and placed them at leading Organizations (MNC, Corporate, KPO, Law Firm) in India and abroad.

Any Organization that invests in R & D, its business policy is heavily influenced by IP related issues and to deal with such issues in an economical, efficient and profitable manner, it is essential for the Organization to train its technical team members in various aspects of IP protection, enforcement and management, which essentially will help the Organization in optimizing the outcome of its R&D efforts.

GIIP's corporate programs have allured R & D team members, scientists, domain experts, IP team members, legal experts from companies, such as, Honeywell, Polaris, TVS Motors, Infosys, ABB, Reliance Industries, GE, Evalueserve, Lexadigm, Panacea, Ranbaxy, KNS partners, Anand and Anand, DRDO, Ministry of IT, CDAC, GAIL, EIL, RITES etc. GIIP has also partnered with IIT Delhi, National Law University Delhi, University of Washington USA, Ministry of MSME, CSIR, CSI, WON (Dutch User Group) to conduct training programs in field of IP & patent laws covering US, EU and Indian jurisdictions

Leadership engagement: Ideas Over a Coffee

Management top leaders at the Director and Vice President level should allocate certain amount of time to encourage 1X1 discussion with idea submitters. If not for all the ideas it should be encouraged at least for the half yearly contest ideas which are of good quality and BUZZ WORTHY. This proves to be a great moral booster for the ideater and gives them the feeling of seriousness of management towards innovation. Not to mistake these discussions for judging the ideas but to be considered to be one sort of an idea grooming and early feedback session. Preferably a cross domain or cross vertical interaction is believed to be more productive and energy boosting than with in the same group. This great opportunity and a straight feedback from a leader who has a good business acumen, can deeply motivate people and there are high chances of them being more prepared for the discussion. On the other hand, management also gets a direct insight about the quality of ideas that are coming from the innovators and decide for themselves for any course correction and pull strings on need basis. Innovation maven should facilitate these meetings and should ensure he communicates the importance of this meeting and the opportunity it brings for both the participants. Also care must be taken to inform both the participants about their contact details and to value each other's time and be punctual if the meeting invite has been accepted. Or otherwise keep the organizer as well as the participants well informed of any schedule changes in the meeting. Healthy Discussions like these proves to be very useful for the idea submitters and they are well prepared for any query that might possibly come from high rank experts during their final idea presentation during the contest judging session. A cup of coffee with some biscuits would add charm to the discussion and make it more casual and transparent.

Involve people managers and product owners in the ideation process. Define Service Level Agreement (SLA) for managers to be part of innovation. Innovation with just a group of people coming together and discussing things becomes a voluntary effort. However, if there is a strong support, push and appreciation from managers, the outcome coming from these innovators is humongous. Managers need to develop a backbone in understanding important role of innovation for organization growth in this fast paced technology savvy world and also understand how big projects (that they value so much on delivering) get shaped from small innovative ideas.

Motivational events

Taking innovators to an unknown location like a mud island or a tree walk where they get to explore their creative skills. They get to learn the basic things in nature on the foundation of which they can build strong concepts. You can also think about reserving a parking lot that says innovator of the week or seat cover for desk chair or inside the bus the employee travels gives a WOW feeling when people are appreciated in front of their colleagues. You can also think about placing down point arrow like placard or a poster that says innovator sits here. Such individuals turns idea creation power houses for the company. Try and see if you can also give onsite exposure to ideater. Such investment would help innovators learn trends in different countries and in the process would not limit boundary of their ideas to a specific geography.

Communications team

Comms team plays a vital role in organizing the events and sending out regular updates on the progress of these events. They are the best people to reach out to in spreading awareness and communicate effectively for the success of the event.

University engagement

University interns are a good source of idea implementers. Work with certain universities and see if you can leverage their talent pool and outsource some of your idea projects for implementation. Outsource few ideas which do not risk technology or intellectual property rights.

Center of excellence

Companies that are serious about innovation attract top talented pool. Apple, Facebook, Google, Amazon, Microsoft are amongst the top innovation companies. Bengaluru based Narayana Hrudayalaya which makes surgery affordable to an average citizen by doing it in mass also competes in the global top 50 innovation list.

Take away

The major benefit for an organization on being innovative is the technology edge over rival organizations.

Innovation cycle

Let's touch base on different stages that are involved in taking your idea from conception to implementation. Here is the listing at a very abstract level.

- **People have ideas**

- Like minded Innovators form a team
- Create a mailing list (or yahoo group) of innovators/champions
- Identify Innovation Leaders / maven to drive the process of innovation
- Create a portal or database where innovators can submit ideas at any time. Simple paper made IdeaBox if there is unavailability of electronics.
- Define different categories in which ideas can be submitted
- Ideas can be an enhancement to existing product or altogether a new proposal
- Have scope for accepting ideas of disruptive nature
- Innovators submit ideas in defined categories
- Reviewing & Consolidating valuable ideas
- Invite active participation to add value to ideas by way of votes, feedback & comments
- Organize weekly sessions to brainstorm on ideas
- Top leaders sponsor events, invite ideas for presentations and rewards valuable ones with a small token
- Active audience help bake ideas with valuable feedback
- Active audience give necessary references to take ideas forward
- Idea submitters work on taking ideas forward
- Implementation is the key - Submitter creates a presentable working model/prototype for his idea
- Leaders identifies similar ideas & help them form a group to create a larger product from small ideas
- Define different qualifying levels for ideas and reward them for crossing each level
- Run theme based half yearly idea competition program like LabRats OR even unplanned/random events on need basis like Hackathon

- **Stake holders interested in ideas, declare cash prize for the competition**
- **Stake holders pick valuable ideas with working model/POC and fund them for completion**
- **Ideas become success stories. Possibly even patentable.**
- **More and more people join the innovation community**
- **With one successful idea, individuals get more ideas**
- **You become an innovation icon**

Innovation in an organization or group

Companies that innovate, thrive. Innovation is crucial to the continuing success of any organization. Innovation brings simplicity and smartness to life. Innovation is to get rid of unwanted things in the system and bring in something that is simple and well received by the people. It need not necessarily be some design change. It can be a suggestive change regarding process (Operational Excellence). At work place encourage individuals to innovate and give them the necessary freedom to step back and look at things and improve them.

Sometimes it's easy to complicate things and sit on it for ages. But it's difficult to make things simpler and efficient.

Organizations should delight customers through rapid innovation and flawless execution.

The best talent in the world is attracted towards innovative companies. Ones that fail to innovate become stagnant and ultimately die in the race of fast paced change. Companies should promote innovation by allocating 10-20% of employee's time towards innovation. Should introduce innovation activities as part of their yearly goals. People managers should develop a backbone for innovation and should encourage innovation coming from team members.

Organization leaders should pay keen attention to ideas that come to their attention and access each one of them with utmost transparency.

It's important to understand that whatever big projects they are currently working on, those are the outcomes of somebody's small innovation done in the past.

Just as the four quadrants of product life cycle are New product, Shining Star, Cash cow and Dogs, every organization should invest in upcoming new ideas and make them grow as a shining star. And at the same time should try to revitalize its cash cow projects by injecting new ideas and making them shining starts again. This will ensure the organizations to stay fit to catch up with the latest trends or challenges that come their way.

"Tough time remains for a while, but Tough person remains forever."

CHAPTER 5

Case study of a global payment company

The Journey

It all started when the organization felt the need of inviting ideas introducing new products and smart techniques along with good user experience to provide value to its customers. There was already an innovation program "**LabRats**" running which was a half yearly innovation contest. It invited ideas in different category but "Tools" category participation was famous. It was a long wait because of its prolonged half-yearly nature. Not many could participate due to prior commitments and devote time as it was completely a voluntary effort over and above your regular job. Regular delivery was still a priority. People wanted something where they could spend their effort in free time. Express their raw ideas instantly as they crossed their mind.

iGnite portal

A portal named "**iGnite**" was therefore launched where employees could submit their ideas anytime and work on them through different phases till completion. This was exciting as we could sense organization's willingness and seriousness towards innovation. We were the early enthusiasts to quickly form a group of volunteers and conduct a meeting and see, how best we can meet the organization expectations about innovation. Around fifty plus people attended the first meeting and everybody felt the need to start the **weekly brainstorming sessions** where people could present their ideas and seek feedback. Thus idea brain storming and grooming weekly **"iGnite session"** was started every Thursday 2PM @ MADLABS. I will talk about this facility MADLABS soon in following chapters.

People started submitting their ideas on **"iGnite"** portal and were eager to know the next step. We quickly spread a word and soon created a distribution list of innovation champions which would automatically get updated as soon as a new person submitted an idea. We also designed a registration page on intranet where people could register their idea presentation slots for the **iGnite sessions**. With this little setup, we reached out to the management and conveyed our interest of driving the innovation effort. We got a go ahead and also blessings to use the MADLABS facility for conducting the iGnite sessions.

iGnite a 24X7 open internal ideation portal for an innovators to submit any idea that comes to his mind, from GoGreen to WiFi on buses. He then works on refining and strengthening it by discussing it with his peers and collecting their feedback. Review committee, continuously monitors these ideas and reach out to submitters for quality ideas. Smaller ideas can become a part of organization's larger initiative. Unique Ideas "that are of organization interest and unique" can be considered for **patenting**. You have to socialize and do a lot of research and collect supportive material to build your idea strong. You can then take this idea for patenting or for the next LabRats event (provided your idea falls in one of the category/theme defined for the LabRats event)

- iGnite is a new global internal portal for all of your hot ideas that aim to add value to our internal and external customers.

- When you comment or make suggestion to help improve an idea, you get rewards.

- iGnite is a collaboration and idea generation portal.

- We have pre-loaded ideas from the past events. Please take time to review them, vote, and add your valuable comments. Good ideas, good suggestions, good discussions spawn more ideas from everyone.

- Go for it!

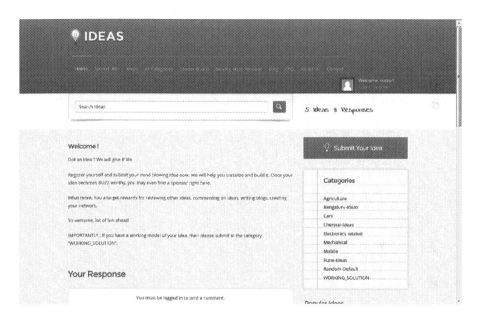

Follow idea submission etiquette

- **A word of caution for all New Idea Submitters.**

- An organization encourages 24X7 idea submission with its portal "iGnite". It simply means, if an idea strikes your mind, the first thing you should do is "submit it". But wait, there is some etiquette that one must follow while submitting an Idea. **Are there similar ideas?**

- Most of the folks who join newly to an Organization come from different geographies and different technological background. With the rich experience they carry and the crisp knowledge that they receive through NewHireTraining (NHT), it becomes very obvious for bright minds to connect the dots and come up with bright ideas that fills the gaps that are present in the current system.

- This is good and welcome gesture but do you know that there is a possibility that someone has already thought through on the same lines? Yes there is a chance that someone has even submitted an idea on the same topic. What do you do?

- **Lesson 1:** Search existing ideas using "KEYWORDS" before submitting any DUPLICATE idea.

- What if similar idea is present but yours is a little different or is an extension to it?

- **Lesson 2:** Team-up with like minded folks.

- Believe me you are only going to get benefited by teaming-up and reap rich knowledge from the fellow idea submitters. Even if a question arises of PATENTING, we have examples where main patent would be in the name of first innovator and the extension of it would be with the second submitter.

- **Lesson 3:** Voice of Customer intranet (http://VOC) is the great source of repository to understand pain points in existing system. Many companies maintain this repository.

- If there is a particular functionality that is bothering and you strongly feel that you have a solve then it is advisable to first browse through some VOC calls around this functionality and see if you can consolidate few more pain points and come up with a holistic solution to address the end user experience end to end.

- Now that you are sure that you surely want to submit one idea but wondering about its content and format to submit? Take help from weekly ideation sessions.

- **Lession 4:** Refer weekly brain storming sessions and the list of ideas presented so far to understand the idea presentation format.

- A NewsLetter that covers the details of ideas presented in the weekly session and gets sent to the innovation group, plays an important role in ensuring that information is reaching to even those who could not participate in the sessions. Also idea presenters feel motivated by seeing their ideas being showcased in the publication.

- **<u>Lesson 5:</u>** Do not spam distribution lists. This way you sure are killing your idea by inviting negative votes from **angry birds**. Follow a protocol by mentioning text in the subject line using which people can filter out your innovation related emails if they do not want to get disturbed during their core working hours. Some text in Subject line as: **[FYI] [iGnite] [LABS]** Use the weekly ideation / brain storming session. Here you have likeminded people coming together and who are open for discussion.

- Now that you are an active member of the innovation team, it become extremely important for you to know what platform your organization provides for innovation.

- I am sure you are now a responsible innovator than what you were, before reading this.

- **Any doubts? Feel free to reach out to innovation champions: Santosh Deshmukh, Sivaraman Sridhar, Raj OS Purushottama, Dhananjay Kumar, Karthik Kastury.**

- **Innovators list: DL-Innovation-Champions-All** to self-join and be part of the innovation community.

- HAPPY INNOVATION!!!

"To succeed don't look at what interests you, know what interests others."

MADLABS

MADLABS (Madras Labs): We got the blessings from the leadership team in form of a facility LAB, where we could facilitate the idea presentation sessions and access to hardware where we can experiment. A nice sitting arrangement with funky colorful walls with adequate dias and TV screens for displaying the presentations.

Organization should have "Innovation & Research LABS" as a separate unit or department that would serve as a center point to drive all the innovation and research programs of the organization.

- It should draw a clear organization's innovation charter with certain milestone that fall in its priorities
- It should build a chasm for bright young minds to connect their thoughts with the organization needs
- It should conduct awareness sessions like:
    - NewHireTraining – To educate on existing framework of innovation
    - MindSpa sessions: On random basis to tap the crowd and bring them in the innovation flow
    - Power Talk series: To educate presenters to make a 3 minute idea presentation pitch
    - How to make your ideas stick session
- It should sponsor funding for implementing valuable ideas
- It should work with media to create the necessary BUZZ about organizations innovation efforts (with help from Communications team)
- It should participate in organizations campus interview drives to tap the right candidates interested in innovation and research

It should work with the communication department for effective communication of the innovation and research programs.

iGnite sessions

We soon started meeting regularly at MADLABS for "iGnite sessions" and exchanging our views on certain ideas that were presented. We also started advertising and attracting larger audience. People from various cross verticals viz Merchant domain, User domain, Application Security, Infrastructure,

Risk, Payments, Money, Data Management, **Product Owners**, Operation Excellence, Compliance and others started attending these sessions. People felt highly motivated to present their ideas in front of this audience and receiving their feedback. Audience on the other hand also felt motivated by attending these sessions and hearing new concepts. People were now able to understand the complete payment system. They started gaining more information and were now able to connect the dots. They could now understand the reason and history behind having different components in the system. They could even sense future needs of customers.

We gracefully stabilized in conducting these sessions.

iGnite session: Weekly ideation/brain storming sessions, that occurs every Thursday 2PM @ MADLABS. This is an attempt to facilitate innovators to present their ideas and seek feedback from the audience. It is also intended to channelize these ideas towards implementation phase and go LIVE. Any queries, doubts, hindrances, roadblocks in moving ideas forward can be discussed during/after the session. Panels from Management, Dev, QA, Product, UED, Application Security, Risk, API, Money team participate in this session and provide their support in terms of technical feasibility and identifying business value for the submission.

NewsLetter

We felt the need of documenting the out come of "iGnite sessions", consolidating the discussion points, audience feedback and communicating it to the group, so that employees remained updated on the ideas that were presented, even if they missed to attend any of these sessions. Thus a NewsLetter for **"iGnite session"** was born. Initially we did not bothered much about the format and sent the details in plain text format and later we started using **Microsoft Publisher** which gave a professional look to the NewsLetter. We even use to take photograph of idea presenters and publish it as part of NewsLetter which truly lifted the motivation of idea presenters. People now felt connected and started contributing more. Till this time there was no investment from organization but just people's voluntary participation. It was just the readily available resources like portal, MADLABS facility, hardware and software that we were using. But the results coming were amazing. More and more ideas started pouring in from the India development center.

Now there was a need to regularly monitor and filter quality ideas and invite only those ideas that would add value to the organization's interest. We identified volunteers who regularly reviewed ideas submitted on portal and invited only those which were not duplicate or incomplete. Thus "**invitation mails**".

Token of appreciation

We requested leadership team to fund small tokens that we could give to the valuable idea presenters. And soon we started distributing coffee MUGS, T-shirts, certificates and batches with nice logo and design that made quite a statement when people kept them at their desk. Idea presenters felt proud to showcase themselves as smart innovators.

Slowly but steadily we created a competition within the community and there were banners, posters, display boards and it gave a complete fresh look to the organization. Ugly old ways of doing things were now thrown back and new approaches were proposed to make life simpler, faster and focused.

Different levels were defined for idea progress and incremental prizes were also given for crossing each hurdle. Everyone looked poised and fully charged with the BUZZ around. The important point to note is that we did not refuse to accommodate any single person who had ideas. Volunteers started working with innovators offline and people now knew whom to reach to if they have ideas.

A pool of BUZZWORTHY ideas got formed and product owners now started coming to the portal and hunting ideas that really made sense for the company. This started generating new work. People were delighted to see their ideas getting implemented by different teams.

A small idea on reducing multiple transaction to just one transaction while you are playing online games or buying music or video items online that was submitted by an engineer, took its shape as a project and almost 250 plus engineers worked on it to make it complete.

There was one more such simple idea where an engineer did just **"one character"** change in his code and that brought 5 million $ revenue to the organization per year. Wondering what exactly the change was? Well the engineer suggested instead of having two digit precisions in calculating fees why not make it to 4 digit precision. eg: So, instead of considering 184.735656 as 184.73 he suggested to consider it as 184.7357. And guess what? Difference of 5 million $ revenue for the organization. Many would argue why keep it to just four digits but then keeping business practices in mind you have to be a little fair.

Imagine you are working on a web browser with multiple tabs open and one of the tab has social networking site open which keeps refreshing all the time and downloads a whole bunch of data, keeping the network and servers busy. You come up with an idea that says "Stop web browser auto refresh for inactive tabs". Small idea but greater potential and impact.

Another such idea that came out from the portal was that of a small Tool built by an engineer that received massive 5K plus hits every day from engineers across all locations of the company.

Some unique ideas caught attention of legal department and they even felt like patenting those ideas.

People from Operational Excellence also were curious to know if they could attend the sessions and pick some valuable ideas which could bring in corrective measure in the existing process and save on time and effort during the release cycle (LIVE to site) of any given product.

People from different cross vertical teams started attending these sessions. Similar ideas were combined and larger products started coming out as the result of our efforts. Ideas that were brought to these sessions were fully baked, more polished, carried greater quality (meat I should say if you are a non vegetarian ☺) and were now ready to compete in any of the company's innovation contest. The half yearly innovation contest "**LabRats**" conducted globally saw many ideas coming from **"iGnite sessions"**. This lead to fierce innovation and people were excited to polish their ideas in these sessions and take them to contest in **"LabRats"**. The contest **"LabRats"** carried a combined prize sum of 65K USD for the teams who win the finals.

Top 5 ideas from different regions like NorthAmericas/Latin America, Europe, MiddleEast and APAC would be selected to make it to the mega show case event at the organization head quarter in San Jose. The winning idea would get the due recognition and the reward in the hands of top leaders. More quality ideas started coming up from APAC region which was the result of our weekly **"iGnite sessions"**. This was noticed by the global leadership team of our company.

I was awarded with the Innovation Award for my efforts towards innovation. Thousand plus congratulatory emails dropped in my inbox. It was a good kick start and a victory well deserved.

Points to ponder:

- Your idea should be explained in as simple words as possible for a layman to understand
- Your idea should have real life examples and simple use cases for the audience to feel the pulse

- You should use **APPROPRIATE-TAGS** ("labsRnD", "mobile", "process", "newgrowth", "patentaval") to highlight your ideas

- Build a repository of people whom you think are interested in innovation and who provide value with their participation. Not everybody likes Steve Jobs ☺

- Reach out to these people for suggestions and getting right references of ProductOwners or domain experts to discuss and promote your idea.

- Keep adding as much supporting material / documents to your ideas available on net.

- Importantly keep answering to all the doubts or queries people post against your ideas.

- Reach out to **Domain leader** that's mentioned against your category of your idea on the portal, mentioned under **MovingYourIdeaForward** section.

Suggestion from Operational Excellence stand point:

What I highly recommend to capture the attention of the judges for idea contest is that you quantify the opportunity benefits. Basically the dollars that the company would save and the number of users impacted and how much of the code that your idea impacts.

For the dollars saved per year you would have to know at least:

- **Number of users impacted**
- **How many approximate hours currently spending do the existing way**
- **How many approximate hours it will take with the new process**
- **$ rate per hour for a user**
- **Cost of implementing the new proposed way**

Seek opinion

Seek people opinion to start process of innovation. People play an important role as main drivers in the process of innovation. They are the ones who understand the core business of your organization and the ones who can judge what is best for your organization.

Call for a general brainstorming meeting and understand the pulse. Ask people in what way they would like to carry forward this process of innovation. Respect their thoughts and help them align their ideas to match a broader perspective of your organization. Engineers may not be able to put their thoughts in correct fashion and here is where you need good leaders to understand the urge of people for innovation and formulate a process that would benefit everyone.

Meeting Minutes: People opinion on starting innovation in an organization

From: Deshmukh, Santhosh
Sent: Friday, February 18, 2011 3:43 PM
To: Global-Innovation-Champions
CC: Global-Innovation-Leads
Subject: MOM: iGnite: Kick start meeting

Hello All,

Thanks a lot for your encouraging response and active participation in the iGnite: Kick start meeting. Here are the meeting minutes that came out in today's discussion:

1. Why is it mandatory to have at least one Full time employee (FTE) in your group as an eligibility criteria for receiving an award.
2. How can one be sure of receiving feedback on BUZZ WORTHY ideas.
3. Some less worthy ideas gets posted. How can we restrict or control such ideas.

4. Should ideas be posted first on iGnite or they are discussed with peers to solidify and align to business need. There is a possibility of someone steeling your idea and posting it before you do.

5. iGnite and LabRats (half yearly competition) program should be controlled or be in sync. Ideas rejected in iGnite were accepted for LabRats.

6. Statistics about how many ideas have made it to completion should be published.

7. Similar ideas should be grouped and a common implementation be brought out to address the business need.

8. Dinner with IDC people (GM/Director/HR) as a reward would be encouraging. People can share their thoughts or bring their concerns to the attention of the leadership team.

9. Weekly session should be started where group of people meet and discuss/present their ideas. People can request for votes in the same session instead of discussing with their peers or friends or sending spam emails.

10. Involve Product team to evaluate ideas on regular basis.

11. Panel should review and decide the value of ideas. Votes should not be the criteria for promoting an idea.

12. People gather votes by simply sending emails to friends.

13. Panel members should be multiple and they should have Business Acumen, Technical aspect, Management view.

14. Panel should be present in IDC to whom people can approach with meeting request and present their idea to take it forward.

15. Feedback on every submitted idea is very important and ideas which is less worthy should be removed from the system.

16. Some incentives should be involved. No matter if the idea is small or big, it should be rewarded if it has a business impact for the organization.

17. An idea is basically an idea which would bring positive gains to the organization.

18. Create an email distribution list specific for iGnite.

I have CCed our Global-Innovation-Leads, who would help us address the above mentioned points.

Looking forward for your valuable support in taking this initiative forward.

Warm regards,

Santosh

> **"Problems can either make you or break you. The hammer that breaks glass can shape steel. It's up to us to be glass or steel! Have A Willpower Of Steel And A Clear Vision Of Glass."**

Organization runs on innovation:

Many of the Organizations stand on the very platform of innovation. One such organization went on to become the global payments company. The whole idea of their product was to have a mechanism where friends can transfer money online, with-in their circle. After achieving transfer of Payments with-in friends, this organization then took payments to a new level enabling transfer between buyers and sellers. Credit card companies being already into this buyer-seller business, this org came up with its unique brand value of **"Buyer Protection"**(assuring refund, if product not delivered or is not as specified) to succeed, which no other funding source provided.

Reward and Recognition

Unique email ids like santosh@x.com are gifted to individuals for their contribution.

Reward idea presenters with something like an ID-card holder or a coffee MUG or T-shirts.

Reward innovation leads with unique identity T-shirts or Hoodey Jackets or Travel bag to keep them motivated and have continuous participation.

Remember, your organization is legally bound and cannot reward contractors with monetary benefits for any noble business idea or even patents for that matter. So don't waste time in banging your head asking for rewards.

Ideathon (Hackathon)

As the name suggest, it's demand based random event creation. You invite ideas which are of interest to your organization. Define various categories and seek ideas in those defined categories. You can predefine these categories on your iGnite portal and make it mandatory to select one while submitting an idea. Also invite ideas on disruptive or random category to not let go any idea for want of category. Voice Of Customer is a great source to understand customer pain points. A regular team walk-through by managers on VOC calls would certainly make people think and come up with innovative solutions, thus leading to more idea submission. Ideas can be invited on different categories like WorkLifeBalance, InternalTools, CommonCustomerPainPoints.

> ***Hackathon / Ideathon:*** Randomly occurring event where a challenge is thrown to different teams of developers to come-up with an application in a stipulated time of 24 continuous hours.

> ***Hack Week:*** Randomly occurring event where a challenge is thrown to different teams of developers to come-up with an application in a stipulated time of one week.

LabRats

This is an half yearly company-wide innovation contest and termed as Spring LabRats, Fall LabRats. Different themes (eg: MobileApp, Digital goods, InnovAsia, Tools) are defined for this contest and Org innovators have to submit their ideas based on the defined themes, as an individual or as a group. Different regions like NorthAmerica, EuropeMiddleEastAfrica (EMEA), Asia, India select their top 5 ideas and send them to the final contest at Org head office in SanJose. Remember, a working proof of concept (POC) is very important. Shortlisted ideas are asked to come up with a POC and the winners are given a bounty cash prize that goes to $ 65K for teams and $25K for individual participation.

Ideas baked on the "iGnite" portal can be submitted to this contest and there are high chances that they win since they are baked and in complete form. Therefore no eleventh hour rushing happens for such ideas. Normally the "LabRats" even will try to define "Disruptive" or "Random" category to tap such ideas but even if these ideas do not fall in the "LabRats" defined categories, **there can be exceptions when your idea has a strong potential and business value.** No organization would overlook a strong business idea. It's a rule that there are exceptions when high stakes are at question.

Shortlisted ideas are asked to come up with a POC and the winners are given a bounty cash prize that goes to $ 65K for teams and $25K for individual participation. Earlier the whole amount was given on winning the prize but then idea submitters started keeping quiet and did not work on completing their ideas. Therefore a new rule was introduced by which 20% of the amount was given on winning the contest and rest 80% was given after complete implementation of the idea. There are certain constraints and challenges that organization faces while rewarding the idea submitters. If you are an full time employee then the organization can straight way extend the reward and benefits to you but if you are a contract employee either through direct contract or through a vendor company then the organizations hands gets tied up in rewarding you because of the company policies and other agreements they have signed with the vendor companies. **In some cases the reward is given to the vendor company and then the vendor company extends it to**

its employee. Therefore it becomes an individual's decision either to submit ideas or stay away from the programs that involve rewarding.

The whole purpose of this contest is to bring in fresh thinking in the existing product line of the company. A car company can't keep making only cars. Company has to balance its product portfolio in order to stay healthy and fit to face the growing cutthroat competition. How many of you know that Madras Rubber Factory (MRF) earlier used to make runner balloons? They then switched to making tyres and MRF is now the biggest tyre manufacturing company in India.

An example idea which has gone through all these phases:

Scenario: An aged person dies due to old age and he has made sure that he has nominated his wife with necessary authority to take control of his assets, insurance and stock investments so that she doesn't face any struggle in case of his death and she is in total control by just producing his death certificate.

On the other hand we have highly qualified couple, both software engineers by profession. Techno savy, with multiple online accounts and relocated to a foreign land for work reasons. The young husband suffers an heart attack one day and passes away, leaving behind absolutely "no clues" for this wife about his property loans, personal loans, bank account, insurance details, stock investments, credit card bills etc. The whole sky falls like hell on this young woman who has to recover from the loss of her husband immediately and take control of the situation even before the recovery agents knocks at her door.

Idea: Having a nominee account in case of person's death. The importance for every individual having it and the consequences of not having it.

I studied RBI guidelines on having a nominee for bank accounts and also downloaded rule books of different bank from different countries. This gives you a holistic picture of what an institution like bank or insurance company should follow in order to ensure safety and security of their account holders.

From this idea you learn that innovation is not always happy, it comes even when you are in deep pain.

You will find:

1. Documents attached which are downloaded from internet
2. More refined wordings to explain your proposal
3. More use cases to make sure that you have been thinking in all possible angles
4. An example of actual requirement something like a VoiceOfCustomer call to support your stance
5. Criticism or challenges brought to notice by reviewers
6. Queries posted by visitors and your satisfactory answers to them

One last important point: **YOUR IDEA SHOULD HAVE VALUE.** If your idea is valuable than you just need to keep baking it up with supporting material, valuable inputs/comments from people and votes would follow automatically without even socializing your idea. This is exactly what happened for my above mentioned idea. **I did not ask for votes** and if you see the vote count now, it has automatically ga**thered 111+ votes**.

On the contrary there is one more idea that I submitted at the very start of **"iGnite"** portal:

Displaying pop-up on your internet page to introduce you to new products that are offered.

And I had to run after every single person to get 85 votes (since it was my first idea and desperately wanted it to succeed)

I learnt a lesson, **YOUR IDEA SHOULD BE VALUABLE.** You should keep submitting as much ideas as possible.

You yourself would get a feel that out of 10+ submitted ideas, only few are valuable. Focus on improving the content/supportive material of those.

HAPPY INNOVATION!!!

AN IDEA CAN CHANGE YOUR LIFE . . .with me . . . it really did . . . 😊

CHAPTER 6

Innovation maven -
Wind cock directions

Identify an Innovation Maven / Leader who should be a polarizing figure. A dedicated person who is passionate about innovation and can be a leading force to drive innovation for your organization at grass root level. He should be a great listener and should be able to inspire people with his own contribution towards the innovation process. He also should have great networking skills and should be honest and trust worthy for people to believe in him and willingly share their raw ideas with him. He should be able to help people in formulating ideas in an understandable format and work with idea submitters on baking them.

Innovation maven ToDo list:

- Email Signature
- DisplayBoard slides
- Posters / Fliers / Standies
- MindSpa session
- iGnite Parking Powered by Innovations Labs
- IDCard hooks with LABS logo

- Modify intranet dev.org.com with Innovations Labs info

- Enough stock of Innovations Labs T-shirts

- Maintaining iGnite connections - this way you get notification on different activities that are happening in your circle and if you can utilize on any of those

- Creating a DL of interested folks - This is important so that you don't SPAM

- Reviewing the ideas on iGnite - This is very necessary and you should be able to pick-up ideas submitted by SJC folks alone

- Sending personal invitation (Ref attach) to present the ideas in iGnite forum CCing submitters managers - This is motivating factor for submitters and also managers can encourage other team members.

- Book presenters MS Outlook calendar if they register their slot for presentation. - This is important and reminder should be 1.5 hours early. This ensures their availability.

- Taking care of filter subject text [FYI] iGnite: -this is important to make sure that nobody complains about your emails as SPAMS

- Also mention in bottom text of email NB: Please add rule to filter PPL emails

- Strictly scold/discourage people of not using DL-Developers-Problem for requesting votes for idea submission. -This way you develop respect and build culture of not SPAMMING. Remember the Christmas MADNESS???

- Maintain consistency in everything you do. iGnite text, invitation mail format, newsletter format etc

- Be present for all iGnite sessions. This is must and you should not be delegating things unless the process streamlines

- Maintain a registration page where people can register their slots to present their ideas. Don't be very strict about this process and give some flexibility since people have tight deadlines on projects.

- Make sure you have registration ahead for two weeks at least

- Present iGnite MUG or some token as a reward for presenting ideas. This should be 1 token per person.

- Be a SPOC for queries and suggestions and an ambassador to promote the initiative
- Decide one day (preferably Thursday 2PM) to have weekly sessions. Monthly doesn't work. Be consistent and do not compromise unless you have an all hands or other important meeting.
- Make sure you are planning for holidays while opening up the slot registrations.
- Apart from invitations, also encourage people to come and discuss their ideas with you before they go for presentations.
- Declare/Ask presenters to present in specific format. Ref intranet Twiki: https://dev.org.com/wiki/General/iGnite
- Create Meeting ID if someone wants to take a call from remote locations and present their ideas.
- Send out a NewsLetter to the DL of interested folks giving them the brief description of each idea and asking them to vote and comment Ref Attach
- Conduct NewHireTraining to promote iGnite sessions
- Conduct MindSpa sessions for creating awareness on how to use iGnite portal
- Create a feedback sheet to understand participants expectations of the sessions and quality of ideas presented
- Try to call people by name and discuss their ideas on personal level
- Make sure you connect them to right folks (like Patricia for Operation Excellence ideas, Mike for Tools ideas) after the session.
- Publish ideas to larger audience (through mail) if they get highlighted or rewarded by higher management
- Send reminder to DL one and half hour early before lunch time to come attend the session. This way nobody misses the session. Thursday 2PM is an ideal time to conduct iGnite innovation session. Friday most of the folks plan to leave for their native or go on a weekend holiday.
- Avoid spamming strictly. Make sure you consolidate multiple things in one single mail as much as possible. Not hampering your regular format of course.

- To complete the process loop, involve product owners who serve as commenters/reviewers and takers for ideas that gets presented.

- Build up a repository with yourself on what different initiatives are ON with-in the organization. You should not spend much time on ideas that are not really important.

- Meet Sr management folks and develop a network with them to get the visibility for your sessions. One word from Sr manager to his folks to attend these sessions makes a lot of difference.

- Your email signature does 90% of the talking for you. Have your location, Extn, Mobile number mentioned there.

- Create a core group of 4+ people who will show up 100% presence to the sessions. So even if you have one presenter, it should appear as if you have more people participating.

- You are the fuel. Keep the fire burning.

- Ref intranet Twiki: https://dev.Org.com/wiki/General/iGnite

Good listener

People need someone to listen to their ideas, even if there is no comment or judgment done. An innovation maven should be the one who can spend time and listen to as many ideas and at the same time keep up with the pace on progress of each idea.

Innovation champions DL

Create a MS Outlook like distribution list of innovation champions which serves a great purpose for effective and smooth communication within the innovation community. This list should automatically get built with names of those who visited your portal. Also give access for people to self-join the DL using intranet **http://dlmanager** tool. Keep building this DL with names of people who attend weekly ideation session. You can have a sheet circulated to catch the names of people who are present. This DL would facilitate easy communication of topics related to innovation. Care should be taken of not creating email SPAM within the organization. A protocol of using specific keywords like [FYI][innovation] in the subject line of an email would help people to filter out innovation related emails. Even if innovation related mails end up in a mail box of a person who does not have inclination towards innovation, there should be a way for him to filter your unsolicited emails. Not everybody likes Steve Jobs.

> **"I can sum up all that I have learnt about LIFE in just three words.. LIFE GOES ON" -Pavan Kopparapu**

Weekly brainstorming session

Start a recurring weekly meeting invite for idea incubation and awareness session. Give a simple but catchy name to this weekly session. This session essentially needs to be a weekly session and not by-weekly or monthly. Conducting this session has to be very consistent with respect to day of week, timing and location. A slight change in any of these can lead to loss of people interest and low turnout. It takes a lot of effort to develop interest among people to attend these sessions and keep them motivated by giving them the feeling of belongingness. Sometimes there will be a very high turnout and sometimes there will be low turnout or even at times you will be the only one present. You still need to keep the momentum going and take corrective measures to see a larger turnout. Calling people by their names and actually sending them a personal note to attend today's weekly session makes a lot of difference. You need to take utmost care of planning for holidays, All-Hands meetings, long weekends. You need to work with HR, Admin staff consistently to avoid any conflict with other organization events or meets. Sometimes even cancelling a session or two, keeping public interest in mind. Don't be afraid to send regular updates emails on these sessions. People who fail to make it due to some escalation or critical issue or other personal work, just love seeing your emails and the ideas being presented on that particular day.

Presence of Product / Business Owners is vital as they are the real buyers of your ideas.

Work with Product / Business Owners and invite them to be part of the innovation sessions.

A Sample meeting invite for iGnite session:

-----Original Appointment-----

From: Deshmukh, Santosh
Sent: Tuesday, December 27, 2011 6:17 PM
To: Global-Innovation-Champions
Subject: [FYI] [iGnite]: iGnite session every Thursday 2PM
When: Thursday, August 30, 2012 2:00 PM-3:00 PM (UTC+05:30) Chennai, Kolkata, Mumbai, New Delhi.
Where: MADLABS

Hello Innovators,

We completed a successful 2011 with 25+ iGnite sessions each packed with mind blowing ideas that qualified for LabRats and actual implementation.

Come 2012, and we are equally poised to continue and drive this initiative with your enthusiastic participation and encouragement.

WELCOME!!! to the 2012 series of **iGnite session** that happens every **Thursday 2PM @ MADLABS**.

This is an attempt to facilitate innovators to present their ideas and seek feedback from the audience.

It is also intended to channelize these ideas towards implementation phase and go LIVE.

Any queries, doubts, hindrances, roadblocks in moving ideas forward can be discussed during/after the session.

Panel members from Arch, Management, Dev, QA, Product, Security team participate in these sessions

And provide their support/feedback in terms of technical feasibility and identifying business value for the submission.

Make use of this opportunity to bring in your BRIGHT ideas and seek expert comments in strengthening them.

Present your idea and you stand a chance to win an iGnite MUG designed by Hollywood actor George Clooney (one MUG per person).

Register your idea presentation slots here: intranet **https://wiki/General/ iGnite**

All presented ideas are communicated to a wider audience in form of a **NewsLetter** to seek more **VOTES**.

Looking forward for your encouraging response as always. Happy New Year!!!

Self-join **DL-Global-Innovation-Champions** using intranet **http://dlmanager**, to receive regular innovation updates.

Santosh Deshmukh | Innovation maven | t: +91.044.663 48347 | Cube: 1.1.145

Submit your ideas & Vote for your favorite ideas on iGnite! --> **http://iGnite**

Note: Please add text "[FYI] [iGnite]:" in subject line to filter innovation forum related emails.

Registration page

Create a registration page where people can book their idea presentation slot. Give them the freedom to cancel or reschedule if at all required. Do not make registration on their behalf instead make it a point that people register themselves. This will ensure that they do not take this invitation for granted and are present for the presentation. Also make it user friendly so that people feel comfortable making changes to their registration slots.

A sample Registration page should look like this:

iGnite: Weekly brainstorming session every Thursday 2 pm (IST) at MADLABS

This is an Idea Incubation platform to encourage and facilitate innovators to present their ideas and seek feedback from the audience. It is intended to connect innovators to product owners, channelize their ideas towards implementation phase and go LIVE. Any queries, doubts, hindrances, roadblocks in moving ideas forward can be discussed during/after the session. Panels from different cross vertical teams like Management, AppSec, Dev, QA, Product, Mobile team, participate in this session and provide their support in terms of technical feasibility and identifying business value for the submission.

Presenters should present their ideas in the following format:

Problem statement : Crisp wordings about the pain point or new functionality that you are planning to propose.

Proposed solution : A brief description about the proposed solution. Graphical representation would be great.

Technical feasibility : Have you thought about the implementation aspect of it and which all areas will be touched in making this change. Backend, WebDev, DB etc.

Legal compliance / acceptance : Have you thought about your idea being legally complaint and would be accepted.

Business Value : What business value your idea would bring to org.

Proof Of Concept if available:

Use case / Real life example (presentation if possible):

Sample Presentation Template: Link.

Intercall Meeting ID: 710032155 can be used to be part of this session, remotely.

Contact Name	Email	Description
Global-Innovation-Champions	Global-Innovation-Champions@IdeaClicks.in	Global-Innovation-Champions list.
Santosh Deshmukh	Santosh.Deshmukh@IdeaClicks.in	Innovation Maven
Sridhar Sivaraman	Sridhar.Sivaraman@IdeaClicks.in	Patent expert
Raj OS	Raj.OS@IdeaClicks.in	Product owner

Registration Table (Book your slot here) – 2012

14 June 2012: Idea presenters of the week

Name	iGnite intranet link	TimeSlot	Idea description in brief
Srikant Kumbhar	https://iGnite.in/Page/ViewIdeas?ideaid=32397	2:00PM-2:20PM	Perl script to extract DB table hierarchy
		2:20PM-2:40PM	
		2:40PM-3:00PM	

Sample invitation mail

Send a personal invitation email to individual idea submitters (CCing his manager) whose ideas you thing are worthy and can be presented in the weekly ideation session. Make sure you are CCing his manager to buy his time for this and at the same time letting him know your praise about the quality of idea his team member has submitted. This is a kind of morale booster and people give their best effort to make presentation as informative as possible. At times managers also put in their efforts to support their team member and make themselves available for the weekly ideation session, thus leading to larger audience. Leave the decision of registration up to the individual and do not force on him. If the person registers for a slot then there are high chances of him presenting the ideas. Sometimes it may so happen that a person books a slot but drops at the last moment. Do not express your displeasure, instead make him feel comfortable by saying it's absolutely fine and maybe he can re-register for any other slot in the upcoming weeks. Ensure that you are not disappointing the audience that come regularly to weekly ideation sessions to listen to ideas. If at all you do not have enough registrations, make sure you have your own ideas lined up to present at such a demanding hour. The subject of these ideas should be mass appealing and should be related to solving the pain points that many of them face regularly. Let people discuss more on the topic and collect their feedback, opinion to give them the feeling of being valued. After all, It's a mind game you are playing. Throw up topics like WiFi on company buses, Minimize usage of paper tissues, Reserve parking for innovator of the month, suspended arrow mark poster at work location to indicate "innovator sits here" etc.

From: Deshmukh, Santosh
Sent: Tuesday, December 27, 2011 3:00 PM
To: Ramachandran, Sujatha
Cc: Venkataraman, Sridhar; Raj OS, Purushothama; sivaraman, Sridhar
Subject: [FYI] [iGnite]: Idea # 24378

Hello Sujatha,

I browsed through your intranet idea **https://iGnite.in/Page/ViewIdea? ideaid=24378** and liked it.

I would request you to present this idea at iGnite: Weekly session @ MADLABS Thursday 2PM and **claim your** iGnite **MUG** (if not yet claimed).

After presenting your idea in the forum we would publish presented ideas in the weekly NewsLetter and send it to **DL-Global-Innovation-Champions** to help you gain more votes.

You can register your idea presentation slot at: intranet **https://wiki/General/ iGnite**

Please feel free to use the presentation template attached to the page.

Calendar booking

Innovation maven browse through and filter quality ideas for presentation. He then sends idea submitters an individual invitation email CC his manager for presenting his idea. Idea presenter responds positively to the invitation mail and registers themselves on the Registration page. Innovation Maven should then book presenter's calendar by sending a meeting invite for reserving their time for idea presentation with 2 hour early reminder. This is important because you discourage others from buying his time during the weekly session slot. Reminding him 2 hours early ensures that the presenter doesn't miss to see his reminder before he leaves for lunch and also gets enough time to prepare for his presentation. Have a professional approach in following this complete process so that people are serious about it and do not bunk their presentation slots and are fully ready with all the material required for their presentation.

NewsLetter

NewsLetter plays a very important role in collaborating all the efforts that go in. You can capture ideas that are presented in the iGnite sessions.

Plain text format NewsLetter: Contains crisp details about the discussion that happened during the iGnite session. Also contains audience feedback and comments. Importantly it must contain the names of **Product and Business Owners** to whom the presenter should reach out to, in order to wet his idea for approval and funding. Don't worry about the formatting. Initially it can go in plain text format. Later you can work on it and decide on a template provided by Microsoft Word or Publisher.

From: Deshmukh, Santosh

Sent: Thursday, January 19, 2012 6:46 PM

To: Global-Innovation-Champions

Cc: Global-Innovation-Leads; Ponnuru, Rajeswari; Ramachandran, Sujatha

Subject: [FYI] [iGnite]: NewsLetter - LABS

Hello everybody,

NewsLetter update on iGnite: iGnite sessions that happens every Thursday 2 PM at MADLABS

We have following ideas presented this week:

Sujatha Ramachandran : intranet **https://iGnite.in/Page/ViewIdea?ideaid =24378 - Time Saving tool - IAS** - Solve the issues & Reduce Execution Time. This tool talks about building a "**RunBook automation**" like process where in you build a knowledgebase for frequently occurring problems and its solution.

This tool is targeted towards reducing efforts especially of new joinees. Engineers need not send email to QA issues DL asking for solution. Submitter needs to work more on making the Tool more intelligent and user friendly. Also spread awareness among fellow engineers to rigorously use this tool and collect their feedback to have a realistic usage experience.

Rajeswari Ponnuru: intranet **https://iGnite.in/Page/ViewIdea?ideaid=25045 - Easy-EMI POS**

This idea talks about org providing easy EMI options to buyers by charging a nominal flat fee in the initial payment. Submitter needs to work more on identifying existing features like BML, the model in which org makes profits. Also, different use-cases needs to be analyzed in which org can make profits.

<u>Ideas Presented so far:</u>

Sai Prasad : **https://iGnite.in/Page/ViewIdea?ideaid=24068**

Technologist Saves Planet (Go Green - Card Readers in our Buses)

Sai Prasad (on behalf of Santosh Vaidyanathan): **https://iGnite.in/Page/ViewIdea?ideaid=21349**

Get Reminder. Get More

More Ideas...

Please take a look and vote positively to promote these ideas.

Those who wish to present their ideas in the next **iGnite** session, please register here:

Registration Link: intranet **https://dev.org.com/wiki/General/iGnite**

You are invited!!!

Note: Please add text "[FYI] [iGnite]:" in subject line to filter **iGnite** forum related emails.

Santosh Deshmukh | Solutions Engineering – Chennai | 1.3.728 | Skype+Gmail: deshmukhsantosh

Microsoft Publisher and available templates.

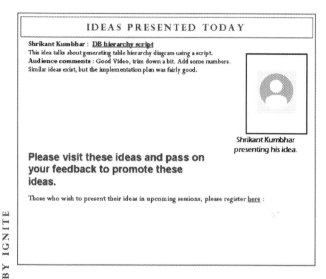

IDEAS PRESENTED TODAY

Shrikant Kumbhar : <u>DB hierarchy script</u>
This idea talks about generating table hierarchy diagram using a script.
Audience comments : Good Video, trim down a bit. Add some numbers.
Similar ideas exist, but the implementation plan was fairly good.

Shrikant Kumbhar presenting his idea.

Please visit these ideas and pass on your feedback to promote these ideas.

Those who wish to present their ideas in upcoming sessions, please register <u>here</u> :

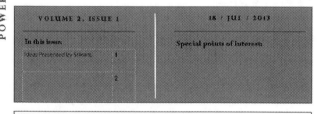

VOLUME 2, ISSUE 1   18 / JUL / 2013

In this issue,   Special points of interest
Ideas Presented by Srikant,   1

                                     2

IDEAS PRESENTED SO FAR

<u>"He who asks is a fool for five minutes, but he who does not ask remains a fool forever."</u>

Email signature

An email Signature plays a very important role in building innovation awareness. Every innovator and especially innovation leads should ensure they are showcasing their inclination towards innovation by displaying an email signature in all their emails within and outside the organization. This attracts people attention and you become easily approachable by means of desk location and contact details and people are sure to stop by your desk to discuss the feasibility of the latest idea they have brewing in their mind. This gives you a chance to be a volunteer or an innovation maven in your organization.

Regards,

Santosh Deshmukh | Solutions Engineering – Chennai | 1.3.728 | Skype+Gmail: deshmukhsantosh

Success stories

Create a list of successfully implemented ideas that came from innovation sessions.

You can showcase your efforts to the leadership team and the difference you are making to your organization.

- List down BUZZWORTHY IDEAS FOR VOTING
- List down fully implemented ideas
- List down Patent idea list
- List down Tools related ideas

  Managers and developers love tools related ideas as they reduce development time and effort and make life easy.

- List down Operation Excellence ideas

Service Management Tool: A UI based user friendly tool used for identifying service dependencies and restarting the services.

This idea was presented in one of our weekly brain storming session by a Jr engineer who had just joined the organization as a fresh graduate. He observed a pain point of engineers struggling every day on stage environment, debugging components, identifying which of their services are not running, and manually restarting the services when needed.

He came up with a small UI based tool which was user friendly and served the purpose. It gave a quick view of a particular services whether it's down or running and also status of all its dependent services. When he learnt about the weekly brain storming sessions happening, he expressed his interest to present this tool to the large audience and seek their feedback to see if it was really useful. No presentations, no beating around the bush but a straight working prototype that he demonstrated which just had one working NodeJS page.

People were excited to know the details. What technology he used to develop it so quickly, and importantly how is the dependency information retrieved. How does he concludes whether a service is actually down or running. How does he restarts the service and its dependent services. Questions even went to an extent of communication protocol being followed, data packets being sent and whether his tool gave 100% accurate results. Poor guy, probably was not prepared for questions of such great length. He simply explained that he decrypted the configuration files from the deployment and read the dependency information and did some polling to conclude if the service was really running or down.

Experts from the audience gave some sharp comments asking him to achieve 100% accuracy and only then publish the tool to the developers. Not otherwise.

We realized that this is a demotivating feedback from the audience and we certainly need to work with this engineer to keep him confident and help him promote his tool. We did so and met him couple of times to share some suggestions and we also encouraged him to add few more functionality to the tool.

The guy was brave and he took all the criticism positively and tried his best to provide the best possible user experience.

The end result was amazing and the tool soon became the necessity of every other engineer to troubleshoot issues and carry out daily testing needs.

Five thousand daily hits were recorded and the tool became HIT in the developer community. People started discussing it on developer problems forum with in the org and started suggesting this tool for monitoring services and restarting them.

Very few knew who the brain and hands behind this tool were.

Backup Processor: Automatically switching between payment gateways to provide uninterrupted payment experience to end users

This one is a real class. An engineer was participating regularly in the half yearly LabRats competition but was unable to catch the attention for the ideas that he submitted. He then came in contact with some of the innovation champions and started attending the weekly brainstorming sessions. His perspective changed after attending these sessions and listening to the questions coming from different angles.

He had never felt the need to socialize his ideas and seek public opinion to see if it would really work. Probably that must be the reason he was not able to articulate it during his presentations. He learnt the tricks of pitching an idea, being precise in using words, time management and importance of bullet points.

He had been witnessing a peculiar customer problem (that of a small grocery stores) which killed most of his and his team's time in trouble shooting the issue and identifying the processor that is down and restarting it. Problem same as above but this was on LIVE SITE and merchants were losing business if one of the processor (amongst twenty nine available) went down. Merchant had to raise a ticket and wait till the issue was fixed cause his merchant account would be mapped to this processor. He had no options but to turndown his buyers because of unavailability of payment processor. The merchant then came up with an alternative of maintaining multiple accounts which probably would get mapped to different processors. So, when one processor would stop responding, he would raise a ticket to fix the issue and mean while, to keep the business going, he would logout with the current merchant account and login with another merchant account which probably would be mapped to different processor which probably must be up and running. He then use to try receiving payments with this new merchant account and keep his buyers happy. But still, this was not the optimal solution as buyers had to wait for some time till the merchant does this switch of seller accounts. Long queues would get formed at the billing counters and people were certainly unhappy.

Knowing all these details and from the past experience of working on issues like these, this engineer came up with an idea and one thing struck his mind, that if merchant can create multiple accounts and switch between processors manually, why can't we achieve this programmatically?

He discussed this idea with the innovation champion group and was almost ready with the solve.

We helped him define a problem statement for his idea and defining the solution that he was proposing.

He did some numbers crunching work with the product owners and came up with a staggering observation that the impact this small idea could make was into millions of US dollars.

People were shocked to know that such a functionality which was so obvious remained unattended for such a long time. He was asked to cut short his presentations and directly work on the fix to push it to LIVE. Not to mention the LabRats award was waiting for him.

He attended the LabRats expo and had a challenging task of presenting this idea to the crowd in a very simple manner. He thought and thought over it and realized it was really very difficult to explain this to the audience. However, he did not give up as it was a million dollar baby. He knew its importance and the only challenge was just to explain it to the audience in a very simplistic manner. Something went through his mind and he started collecting things. Placed in a hotel room, he brought all possible things from the market. Stickers, thermocol, plastic etc. Then he again went to the market and came back with a rail track and a wooden ball.

He was ready. He threw everything aside and just stuck to the rail track and the wooden ball. He created one main track and one alternate track if the ball on the main track did not go through and hit a dead end and came back. The ball would then take the alternate path and reach the target.

This was the exact replica of his processor idea. If the payment did not go through with the first processor, an alternate path of another processor would be taken and the payment be completed successfully. Hushhhh . . .

***"I am proud, I stand away from the crowd"* –Santosh Deshmukh**

Advertise

Create innovation presence on company intranet homepage. Companies generally have an intranet home page which is most frequently visited by employees. Having an innovation portal link on this page can help us gain attention in a big way.

Distributing MUGS, T-shirts, stickers that creates BUZZ.

Crystal ball / Display boards / Standies / Notice boards

Arrow marks

Show large arrow marks (created with blotting paper) from false ceiling indicating, Innovator sits here.

Volunteers

- Create a Distribution List/Group of volunteers who are willing to put additional efforts for building a POC of any idea. Something like DL-iGnite-STF (special task force)
- Insist on having a POC to all idea submitters
- A working model has a greater impact when you present it to the business or product owners. There are high chances of getting a quick buy-in for your idea.
- Just talking about ideas and not creating a POC <u>creates a very void impression</u>
- Ideas, brainstorming, and most critical prototypes & execution!
- discuss over the possibility of taking the shortest possible routine for implementing small ideas with greater benefits
- I have identified few **ideas (around 10) which are low hanging fruits** and easily doable with few modifications and reusing the existing functionality.

- **Few folks from Dev, web-dev, qa expressed their interest on working small iGnite ideas driven projects like these.**
- These are the folks who closely work with a particular product and has better knowledge on how the customer experience should be.
- Talk to executives and get their buy-in for funding such initiatives.
- Have a plan to form a **DL-iGnite-STF** (SpecialTaskForce) which consists of passionate developers who are ready to contribute extra time and effort to get iGnite ideas implemented.
- Love to lead the effort and enhance the product with better customer experience. Tasks can be created and assigned through Rally tool to individuals of any location.

Ideas keep getting submitted into the portal and people bake them by presenting them in the weekly session, discussing with fellow colleagues and friends. These baked ideas need a showcasing platform where they can compete with other ideas and prove their quality. Organize a half yearly Spring LabRats and Fall LabRats contest and define categories that are of interest to organization business. People who have submitted their ideas so far on the innovation iGnite portal can move their ideas to these newly defined LabRats categories and be a part of the contest.

Quick wins / Low hanging fruits

The sole idea behind forming this group is to identify and consolidate ideas which are QUICK WINS from Org perspective.

These ideas come from people who are closely working with the product for couple of years and strongly feel that implementing them will have a HUGE customer experience improvement.

Anybody can be a part of this initiative either to come-up with the proposal or for voluntarily implementing it.

Submitter	IdeaClick intranet link	Idea description	Volunteer name	Status
Abhilash	https://iGnite.in/ ViewIdea?ideaid=23806	Sitespeed reduction by 2 minutes		

"In the name of development, we are rushing towards destruction."

–Santosh Deshmukh

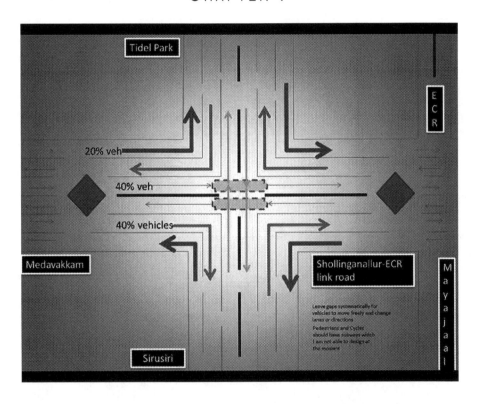

Traffic Signal Solution without flyover: Six lanes to bifurcate some part of the traffic early i.e even before it comes to the crossing point.

Author's ideas

- Digital display boards in conference rooms which are integrated with MS Outlook and displays current bookings and avoids conflicts between fellow co-workers.

- Start a KonBanegaCrorepati (KBC) like technical quiz on TV hosted by a techie like Sabeer Bhatia

- Create collapsible curtain compartments in SUV like cars (with heat non-transferable material) to avoid unnecessary air conditioning of entire cabin space thus saving on fuel.

- Create a hand-brake like lever which can be used to move your car forward or backward in case of a breakdown.

- Design a wrist watch which can run both clockwise and anticlockwise

- Create a marketplace for farmers where farmers can list their produce and buyers can buy it. The intention is to exclude the middleman from taking the big profit cut.

- Exposing an API for authentication using a UNIQ-ID. We have to create account at various sites that we visit and keep adding our basic details every time. The idea is to create one website say MyProfle. com that captures all your personal, medical, passport, bank details and exposes these details by way of an API to the external world. Then integrating with different sites and accessing your details using your UNIQ-ID from MyProfile.com. This way you will not have to remember your userID and password and one single UserID & Password can be used at all the site where there is an integration between MyProfile.com and the website. Something like Login with FB or g+. Point to note is that it would be every users discretion as to how much of information he wish to make public and how much he wants to keep private.

- Design a vehicle using which you can offer a lift/ride to anyone without allowing him to get in to your car cabin. This will reduce traffic on road quite considerably and at the same time raise social awareness "giving".

- Create a remote door locking and unlocking system using internet or mobile app which can be used to provide access to your apartment if you are renting it out to a tenant or provide access to your "**Home Safe**" to a trusted person.

- Tollfree ride for cars that have occupancy to its capacity. This would encourage people to offer rides to others thus leading to reduced traffic on the roads. Ofcourse double toll for those who go empty. Otherwise the private companies collecting the toll would suffer.

- Six lane design to solve the traffic signal problem without using flyovers. Idea is to bifurcate some part of the traffic even before it hits the actual crossing point and reduce the bottle neck there by keeping the vehicles moving. Then dealing with the remaining traffic by designing a circle at the crossing where vehicles converge and diverge. Also part of the idea is to get rid of flyovers and encourage walking as much as possible cause managing vehicles incurs a lot of cost where as walking crowd manage themselves. Encourages good health.

- Create a social networking site www.MyChoice.com where you can share your likes especially the items you prefer in your daily use. So, just as we have some fan following the celebs, there would be people following on what others prefer and buy. This will help us to follow those who love class apart products. For eg: If I as an individual, is very particular about the products that I use and does enough amount of research before deciding on one particular brand, then people in my friend list would love to check my profile first if they are planning to buy a particular car or bike or any luxury item like a wrist watch. They know that the decisions I make have enough substance and it surely has to be a great product. This will encourage people to buy more and more things. I can maintain a healthy portfolio of the items that I buy and keep updating it with the latest purchases. Even companies would start approaching such individuals and only authentic and proven products would sustain in the market. Right now there is so much of confusion and misleading done in the market. If I have to buy a water purifier, I am just lost and do not have enough time to actually go into minute details of each and every provider. So the best thing I would do is, check my friend's profile on www.MyChoice.com and take a call on what to buy. The concept is a little different from the normal product rating sites. There you have a general public mandate but this is strictly following one particular person's choice.

"All change is not growth, as all movement is not forward."

~Ellen Glasgow

External avenues

Once you develop the mindset for innovation, you naturally start getting more and more ideas. Let those ideas come. Don't restrict them to just your organization needs but also give your brain a freedom to cross all boundaries and think of innovating all that is around. Participate in external contests and evaluate your brain power with the real competent innovators around you.

Creative Commons: http://creativecommons.org/

A nonprofit organization that enables the sharing and use of creativity & knowledge. It has, easy-to-use copyright licenses provide a simple, standardized way to give the public permission to share and use your creative work — on conditions of your choice. Creative Commons licenses let you easily change your copyright terms from "all rights reserved" to "some rights reserved."

Khan academy: Videos are available on https://www.youtube.com which are meant to teach different subjects. The intention is to deliver the same standard of teaching to every child in the world which Bill Gates' son must be getting.

Maruti-Suziki: WagonR think BIG challenge: http://www.wagonrsmartideas.com/

Economic Times: Power of Ideas: http://www.ideas.economictimes.com/

Mahindra: http://www.sparktherise.com

National Innovation Council: http://www.nic.org

NABARD Rural Innovation: http://www.nabardruralawards.com/

Forbes: World's Most Innovative Companies – 2012

http://www.forbes.com/special-features/innovative-companies-list.html

Most of the top innovative companies like Apple, Facebook, Google, Amazon work extensively towards maintaining a healthy Patents portfolio in order to control the competitive advantage over rival companies. In such process some also go to an extend of acquiring smaller organizations and buy their patents in the deal. There are few organizations which believe in homegrown Patents and invest more on innovation and research activities.

Innovation Penal Code (IPC)

We would explain certain rules that should be followed as standard guidelines in the process of innovation. Certain do's and don'ts that might impact the initiative. How the competition should be kept healthy to generate more and more ideas by creating an atmosphere of positivity and togetherness. If these rules are followed due diligently by event organizers or organizations there are bright chances of gaining people trust and succeeding in the process of innovation.

Section 1: Treatment towards innovators

a) Motivate innovators for idea submission but do not mandate them or take a stick approach on submitting ideas. This way you would quantity of ideas but not quality in ideas.

b) Do not cheat innovators by stealing quality ideas from them in exchange of false promises or some low priced freebies. Such acts should be treated as criminal offense and be dealt with harsh punishment. At any point if innovators feel cheated, it would result in losing trust and transparency.

c) There should be utmost transparency maintained while handling the ideas throughout its life cycle to show the idea progress and the final outcome of the submitted ideas. Failure to which can result into demoralization of interest, which can hamper the trust factor build on the innovation community.

d) Duplicate ideas should be identified by way of opinion poll or votes and should be shown no leniency on closing them.

e) Contract should be declared before inviting ideas from innovators and necessary due credit should be given to innovator for sharing his idea. Failure to do so should be treated as criminal offense and be dealt with harsh punishment.

f) Written proof or communication details should hold good for one to claim and file a patent.

g) Extension on any innovation and the benefits it bears should be treated independently and there should be no sharing of profits whatsoever with the actual innovator.

Section 2: Idea submission etiquettes

a) Innovators should first search for similar ideas if at all present (by means of keyword search) before submitting any new ideas to avoid duplication.

b) Innovators should possibly team-up with existing ideas if at all their idea matches to some extend with the existing idea and by mutual agreement should share the benefit that comes along.

Section 3: Patent filing

a) Seasoned Innovators who have bunch of ideas and think they would click, must ensure that they patent those ideas by seeking help from legal lawyer firms. For this an innovator and lawyer firm must first sign a legal contract, a non-disclosure agreement and then on completion of this agreement process, innovators should reveal his ideas to the lawyer firm in form of a template document or an idea submission form. The agreement firm then should assist the innovator in performing a search whether there is already a patent filed for such an innovation and if not should help the innovator filing a successful patent. There are certain fees applicable for doing a patent search and actually filing a patent.

"Before you start with something. Always ask yourself. At the cost of what?" –Santosh Deshmukh

CHAPTER 8

Daily life innovation

Do a quick search on the internet for **"sawantwadi wooden toys photos"** and see the images tab, you would see innovation at its best. It depicts the story of a small town Sawantwadi in Sindhudurg District of Maharashtra state in India which is famous for wooden toys. It takes innovation to create every single toy, right from spinning tops, motor cycle, cars, crocodile, dancing dolls, chess boards, birds, fruits, colorful hanging show piece matt to different models. Thanks to the wood craft industry which is still active here. The above photograph is the one I took when I visited this place (aka SunderWadi) last year and was stunned to see the creativity.

Living With Elephants is an initiative in Valparai, Tamilnadu state of India where people are alerted through, cable television network, SMS, Flash Lights about the movement of elephants (both at night and day), thus avoiding the encounters which was resulting in human deaths. Valparai has a population of nearly 100 elephants which lives around tea plantations. Unfortunately every year people get accidentally killed by these elephants.

Another story of a person from Coimbatore who came across a basic problem that most of the women face during their periods. He observed that unhygienic, useless or dirty cloth are used instead of sanitary napkins because of the affordability factor. He realized sanitary napkins contains raw material which is not so expensive but still companies sell it for higher price. His research went for more than two and half years in order to meet the standards of sanitary napkins in the market.

He decided to prepare a low cost machine which can be given to any village and women can bring their own raw material and prepare sanitary napkins for themselves. He ensured that his solution was practical, affordable and benefiting many.

There are multiple innovative people like these who innovate in their respective fields.

A stranger approached an 8 year old girl and asked her to come with him. The stranger told her that something had happened and her mom had sent him to pick her up. The girl asked the stranger for the PASSWORD and used the man's confusion to run away. She and her mom had agreed to a PASSWORD in case she had to send someone to pick her up. This saved the girl's life. A simple and easy thing to do.

During monsoon rains a heavy landslide occurred on a busy highway and the traffic came to a stand still. Taking note of the situation a local fellow asked his wife to prepare some hot samosas (a local snack in India) and masala tea. He took this to the highway and people started ordering him and the stock started flying in bulks.

Same thing happened when a celebrity status cabinet minister was arrested in a fodder scam case and was put in a remote jail. Earlier, hardly anyone would visit this place but after the minister's arrest thousands of political leaders along with their followers started visiting this place, to discuss crucial matters with the minister. The result was, villagers noticed this spur and few early birds were quick enough to put their pan stalls to sell tobacco, cigarettes, mineral water to the visiting crowd. With small investment, they were able to make lot of money.

Politicians can have ideas on winning elections and each year we often see them coming up with innovative approaches to lure their voters. Some distribute television sets, some distribute laptops and bicycles for college students while some take the elderly people on pilgrimage.

Students have smart ideas on how to skip homework and still escape scolding.

Auto rickshaw drivers have innovative ideas on how to beat the traffic jams and reach the destination.

Train commuters or bus passengers find innovative ways to reserve their seats. How many of you use your handkerchief to reserve a seat for your friend?

Naughty students in Mumbai running to catch their train have innovative way to disperse the platform crowd by shouting "MACHI KA PANI", "MACHI KA PANI" (FISH WATER GET ASIDE) scaring people and making way for themselves. **Innovation is as simple as this.**

A group in Mumbai, decided to punish those who urinate in public. Armed with a yellow water tanker, water hoses and covering their identities with masks this group roam around Mumbai with a water tanker named as 'The pissing tanker', and attack the offenders with a giant water cannon, which indeed makes for a funny sight for onlookers. Their motto is simple 'You Stop. We Stop'.

Innovation has its chance of being present in almost every difficult situation. The Indian air-force when assigned a task of evacuating stranded pilgrims in Uttarakhand during the monsoon floods, they had to use their choppers for the rescue operation and there was quite a possibility of air collision in the tough terrain which had very low visibility. Also refueling these choppers was quite a task since the base station where refueling can be done was quite far from the actual site. The bright minds in the air-force step back for a while and realized the complexity of the situation and came up with a simple approach to follow a protocol of flying right side of the valley and close to the mountain so that the up-coming chopper doesn't cross the path of on-going chopper and thus avoiding the possibility of air crash. They also brought in a refueling chopper which had high storage capacity and could help in refueling the choppers on duty without necessarily going the long way to the base station.

These are simple things which every individual can come up in the hour of necessity.

There are some examples of social innovation which would have an impact on life of masses.

Gandhi Ji introduced Satya and Ahimsa an innovative way to fight the mighty British power in India and South Africa to gain freedom. This innovative way called Gandhi giri went global and became way of life to many.

Aryabhatta introduced ZERO in the number system which is accepted globally. Such is the power of innovation that you can bring in a massive change in the life of people.

Karnataka's KSRTC bus service was running into losses because of the low mileage of their buses. A smart engineer proposed to change the flat front face of the bus to an aerodynamic shape, thus leading to better mileage and huge savings. You would notice, even boats and ships have an angular shape to cut through the water pressure and move ahead.

Sometimes, the solution is right next to us. We just need to connect it to the problem that we are facing.

Remember the movie Chillar Party? There is a struggling young man who has a natural weakness of having a female like voice. He gets rejected wherever he goes job hunting. People in the society look down towards him and avoid him. Completely dejected and depressed having no clue on what to do next. That is when a small kid working as domestic help in his housing society, cleaning cars, walks to him and asks "Why don't you become a radio jockey?, Nobody would know whether it's a male or a female behind the mic". Brightened, this young man turns his weakness into his strength and goes on to become the most popular RJ in the town.

No matter how big a person you are, you may have to learn from a person smaller than you.

Such is the power of ideas and it can change one's life.

The more you use your brain, the better it gets. One cell in our brain is more efficient than a computer. And we have such brain cells in trillions. People who make most use of it, grow faster in life. One doesn't need to be smart, one can become smart.

Look around and think what I can do better. Step back at times and see what I can do differently in a given situation. There are many problems around us and enormous opportunities to pick and make a difference. Early birds sense it early and make the most out of it.

India's captain MS Dhoni tells his boys, don't look up. God is not going to come and help. You have to take action to see the match results. Same message holds good for all the innovators out there. And I am going to emphasize more on taking the lead in getting things done and making the difference.

Revolutionary Ideas

Ganesh Festival: Lokmanya Bal Gangadhar Tilak a freedom fighter and great leader, felt that there was lack of unity amongst the Indians and this was a major drawback to fight the freedom struggle against the British rule. He therefore came up with an idea of bringing the elephant God Ganesha from his worship room to the street and let everybody participate in worshipping the lord instead of him doing it alone. This idea was mainly to unite youngsters by involving them in various activities related to the festival. Activities like performing prayer, playing music, distributing Prasad, dancing, performing drama etc. This idea became so revolutionary that even today cities like Mumbai and Pune celebrate this festival in a very grand manner.

India and Global Innovation Index 2014

- India slipped 10 notches on the Global Innovation Index (GII) 2014. India fell from the 66th position to the 76th on the index.

- India became the only one among the BRICS economies that fell in the rankings of countries based on their innovation capabilities.

- China was the best among BRICS nations at 29th position, an improvement of six places. Russia went up 13 places at 49th rank. South Africa ranked 53rd, went up five places, while Brazil at 61st position, moved up three places.

- The divergence of India from the rest of the BRICS economies is the result of the challenges it faces in integrating its efforts along the different dimensions of innovation to sustain a high level of innovation success.

Prime minister speaks

India's prime minister calls for 'innovation ecosystem'

Mr Singh says, "Innovators must be challenged to produce ground breaking solutions that our society needs"

India should have an "innovation ecosystem" to drive the country's development over the years to come.

Singh called for an environment in which scientific establishments, industry and agencies provide start-up funds for innovative ideas and newer products.

India's planning commission, which develops five-year roadmaps for the country's economic growth, set up an innovation expert group in 2009 to identify sectors where innovation could help India achieve more inclusive economic growth.

But much more needs to be done, Singh said.

Indian scientific establishments, including the Indian Institutes of Technology (IIT), must change their mindsets to promote an innovation culture, said Singh.

For example IIT's research goals should be aligned with the expectations of the industrial and social sectors, while Indian scientific institutes need to improve their "outward orientation" by strengthening links with industry and increasing international research partnerships.

Ideas should be crowd sourced in the field of Solar energy and water resources management.

"Victory loves preparedness.?" – Behind enemy lines.

Inspirations

Mr. Satyanarayan Gangaram Pitroda popularly known as Sam Pitroda, speaking on Indian Innovations as the Chairman of National Innovation Council, India:

http://www.youtube.com/watch?v=6Ax5i3YQaLA

Meet Sridhar Sivaraman: A bright and innovative Software Professional working with us who has six successful patents to his credit.

Details link: http://patents.justia.com/inventor/sridhar-sivaraman

CHAPTER 9

Patents by Inventor Sridhar Sivaraman

Right Click Electronic Commerce Transactions

Application number: 20140032320

Abstract: Embodiments of the present disclosure provide a right click transaction option and enhance the e-commerce experience In an embodiment, a system comprises a processor(s) and one or more memories in communication with the processor(s) and adapted to store a plurality of machine-readable instructions which when executed by the processor(s) are adapted to cause the system to: provide a right click transaction option as part of a right click context menu when a user of a client device right clicks on content associated with a selected item as presented on an entity's site; receive search information associated with the selected item from the user device when the user selects the right click transaction option; store the search information; and redirect the user to a service provider site of a server provider showing one or more items displayed from service provider supported business entities based on the received and stored search information.

Type: Application

Filed: July 24, 2012

Issued: January 30, 2014

Assignee: eBay, Inc.

Inventor: Sridhar Sivaraman

Interactive Television Shopping Via A Payment Provider

Application number: 20130347013

Abstract: A television viewer can shop for items related to a particular television program through use of a payment provider. The viewer can request that a search be performed for program-related items. The results of the search are then displayed to the viewer on the television screen. The viewer can then select items to be purchased and place them into a virtual shopping cart on the television screen. Payment for the items is then processed by the payment provider.

Type: Application

Filed: June 22, 2012

Issued: December 26, 2013

Assignee: eBay Inc.

Inventor: Sridhar Sivaraman

Wish List Transactions Through Smart TV

Application number: 20130325644

Abstract: A user may create a wish/gift list and send the list to recipients, who have the option of accepting the list. Content being viewed or recorded by recipients who have accepted the list is scanned to determine whether the content is relevant to one or more items on the list. If so, an alert is displayed on a recipient device, which can be the same device as the displayed content. The recipient may select the alert to purchase the item(s) or obtain additional information about the item(s) for a subsequent purchase.

Type: Application

Filed: August 23, 2012

Issued: December 5, 2013

Assignee: EBAY INC.

Inventor: Sridhar Sivaraman

Friendly Funding Source Messaging

Application number: 20130268435

Abstract: A sender can request payment of a third party invoice by messaging a receiver. The receiver may accept or deny the payment request. The request to pay a particular invoice may be sent via a sender through an on-line request, electronic mail and/or text messaging to a receiver who may have an account with an on-line payment provider. Upon receiving the request, the receiver may accept or decline the payment request via electronic mail and/or text messaging. If the receiver accepts the payment request, the amount of the invoice is deducted out of their on-line payment provider account.

Type: Application

Filed: April 10, 2012

Issued: October 10, 2013

Assignee: eBay Inc.

Inventor: Sridhar Sivaraman

Shared Mobile Payments

Application number: 20130159173

Abstract: Methods and systems are provided for facilitating shared mobile payments. According to an embodiment, a user can initiate a purchase using a mobile device. The mobile device can display a total price for the purchase. The first user can cooperate with one or more second users to share the cost of the purchase. The cooperation can be facilitated via the first and second users' mobile devices.

Type: Application

Filed: December 19, 2012

Issued: June 20, 2013

Inventors: Sridhar Sivaraman, Venkata Brugubanda

Method for Authorizing the Activation of A Spending Card

Application number: 20120296818

Abstract: A method of authorizing the activation of a card holder's spending card is provided. The method includes receiving a request from the card holder to authorize the activation of the spending card and then requesting identity verification of the card holder. Following the identity verification request, the method includes obtaining a geographic location of the card holder. After determining the geographic location of the card holder, the method may include temporarily activating the deactivated spending card and instructing the card holder to conduct at least one transaction with the spending card at at least one selected location, wherein the selected location is selected based on the geographic location of the card holder. Spending card activity may be monitored to determine whether the at least one transaction was completed, and, based on whether the at least one transaction was completed, the activation of the spending card may be authorized.

Type: Application

Filed: May 17, 2011

Issued: November 22, 2012

Assignee: eBay Inc.

Inventors: Frank Anthony NUZZI, Sridhar Sivaraman

"Be the change that you want to see in the world." -Mahatma Gandhi

CHAPTER 10

Innovator Award

Ref: in.linkedin.com/in/santoshdeshmukh/

"Santhosh volunteered to be the innovation maven in PayPal's chennai office. His rigorous efforts and organization skills created awareness of a new internal ideation portal among 37% of the staff at chennai location within 6 months.

He organized innovative idea review/evaluation session for over 30+ ideas, attended regularly by 250+ Paypalians.

He is a passionate contributor towards innovation efforts within Chennai office." *September 6, 2011*

(1st) Shahid Khan, *Innovation Evangelist & Coach, PayPal*
managed Santosh indirectly at PayPal

Signoff

I would sincerely like to thank you for showing interest and choosing this book to take a deep dive in understanding an important topic like innovation. I hope the content of the book was fulfilling and satisfying to your expectation.

However, if I have missed something, please feel free to drop me a note at deshmukhsantosh@gmail.com with "[IdeaClicks]" as the subject line. I would certainly try to accommodate valuable topics that would enrich the quality of this book. With this note I take your leave. Happy Innovation!!!